The Travel Scam Survival Guide

[2018 Edition]

Peter John

Oakamoor
Publishing

Published by Oakamoor Publishing, an imprint of Bennion Kearny Limited

6 Woodside
Churnet View Road
Oakamoor
Staffordshire
ST10 3AE

www.BennionKearny.com

About the Author

Peter John is a lifelong traveller who dabbles in office work while planning his next trip. He has never knowingly scammed anyone, but has been scammed while he travelled more times than he cares to remember. He hopes that others can learn from his mistakes, which are spelled out in merciless detail in this book.

Table of Contents

Preface

By December 2009, I had been travelling, on and off, for seven years, visiting dozens of countries around the world. Towards the end of that month, I was staying in the city of Tulum, on the Yucatan peninsula in southern Mexico, between Belize City and Cancun. It is famous for its Mayan ruins, its *cenotes,*[1] and its wide, sandy, white beach. I had just come back from an entertaining day snorkelling and swimming with the turtles which are often to be found a few yards offshore. After returning my snorkelling gear to the front desk of the hotel where I was staying, I bought a bottle of water and sat in the open common area.

On the next table was an English couple who were travelling south through Latin America. We started talking almost immediately, as travellers do when they are not going anywhere in particular. They had started in Mexico City and had allowed themselves six months to reach the southern tip of Argentina. Almost three months into their trip, however, they were still in Mexico. I wondered why. They had had a disaster in the first few days of their trip which meant that they had needed to remain in Mexico to resolve it. Over an hour or two, while watching the dying sun and trying to protect my bare skin from the mosquitoes, I slowly wormed the story out of them.

It seemed that they had arrived in Mexico City, stayed a few days, and then booked a bus ticket to the next town on their itinerary. They had arrived early, and had been sitting in the bus station, waiting to leave. Bus stations in Mexico can be very busy indeed, and there are usually no restrictions on who is allowed in. People in bus stations often carry all their possessions with them, including valuables. They are perfect for casual thieves, two of whom had apparently targeted my new friends, who had been sitting with their backpacks on the ground next to them. One of the thieves had thrown what looked like a baby, but which was, in fact, a doll, at one of the couple, and the other had snatched their backpacks. The thieves had simply disappeared into the crowd, and nobody else had seen a thing. The couple had lost their cameras, clothes, toiletries, credit cards and some cash. Most annoyingly of all, they had lost their passports. Had they just been visiting Mexico, they would have been able to buy emergency passports from the British embassy in Mexico and fly back home. However, because they were travelling down South America, they needed to buy new 'complete' passports. As the British Embassy in Mexico had no printing press, they had to get passports sent to them from Washington, D.C. This turned out to be a nightmare because the embassy was always sending them to the wrong place. Ten weeks after losing their passports, they were still waiting for them. It had seriously affected what they had thought would be the trip of a lifetime.

This couple's story caused me to reflect on the lengths to which people, companies, and even certain governments will go to gouge money from travellers without offering goods or services in return, or offering only inadequate goods or services – ripping them off, in other words. Tourists are often regarded as about the softest targets by the unscrupulous and the amoral. Some of their schemes are so ingenious as to be wonderful, in a twisted way. During my travels, I had, of course, heard many stories of scams and rip-offs, legal, barely legal and illegal. I had indeed fallen for some myself, though I had not suffered any major disasters. However, I thought that others might benefit from details of the more common tricks, and decided to set down what I had heard and experienced in writing. Guidebooks to individual countries often warn of scams when they are covering a particular country or tourist attraction, but their coverage is rarely as comprehensive as it should be.

What follows, therefore, are over sixty travel scams which people have suffered, either before travelling, while travelling, or after they have reached home. They have been compiled following that fateful meeting in 2009 and made fully up-to-date for travel in 2018 and beyond.

Note:

[1] A *cenote* is a sinkhole with exposed, rocky edges, fairly common on the Yucatan peninsula. The Maya believed that they were gateways to the afterlife.

Introduction

This is a book about dishonest people trying to get at your money when you travel. It is about how they do it, and how to try to stop them. Reading it will mean that you are better prepared to resist scammers and their scams, though it cannot ensure that you will never fall for another scam while you travel. Scams are like viruses; they mutate all the time. As soon as people develop resistance to one strain of a scam, thieves devise another.

Ripping off tourists is a way of life for many people in certain countries, and for some people in just about every country which receives any tourists at all. An important message from this book is that many scams are not perpetrated by dodgy young men in bars or people who send you scamming emails. Often, governments join enthusiastically in discriminating against, and exploiting, travellers, and do so unashamedly. Just because their scams are legally enforceable does not make them right.

As I repeatedly stress, travellers are easy victims. People are often more laid back when they travel. Finding scams which are targeted at travellers, or from which travellers suffer disproportionately, was much easier than I thought it would be. I had experienced many myself while travelling. I had also met plenty of other travellers who had been ripped off in lots of different ways. Newspapers, magazines, and the Internet provided the remainder.

I do not want to discourage people from travelling at all. If that is what this book does, it will have failed in its purpose. I aim to make people more confident to travel. Despite all the scams and other, minor annoyances, travel is (for just about everybody) a hugely rich and rewarding experience - whether it is the annual package holiday on a nearby beach or a year-long round-the-world adventure. The number of holidays that end in disaster or serious inconvenience is *tiny*, and many catastrophes can happen at least as easily at home as overseas.

Structure of the book

The book describes 66 scams, organised thematically into ten chapters. My descriptions of each scam include two scores by which I rate the scam:

The first judges the scam out of five, by how damaging the direct effects of the scam are likely to be to the victim or victims. A rating of one indicates that the victim is likely to lose $25/£20 or less. Two shows damage of between $25/£20 and $250/£200. Three indicates likely financial costs of more than $250/£200. Four shows that the victim is likely to be physically harmed, and five means that the victim is in serious danger of going to prison for a long time or of losing his life.

The second value scores the scam out of five in terms of how probable it is. A traveller will be very lucky to avoid a scam rated five in a country where it is widespread, but would have to be very unlucky to experience a one-rated scam.

Inevitably, both these ratings are somewhat arbitrary and unscientific.

Moving on, I provide additional information including:

- Where possible, the locations where I believe a scam to be most prevalent (though many of the scams I describe can happen just about anywhere).

- A summary of the scam.

- A full description of the scam and its most common variants.

- How best you might avoid becoming a victim of the scam.

- Where possible, examples of the scam. Some examples are from my own experience, and others are from people for whom I can vouch. Others, again, are from newspapers, government websites or web forums.

After the descriptions of the scams, I end with a dozen general tips for avoiding many of them, based on my own experience.

Chapter 1: Hotels and other accommodation scams

Accommodation is most people's largest expense when they travel. Great hotels or mountain lodges can be a great feature of any trip. Many travellers are ripped off, however, by being offered substandard (sometimes non-existent) apartments or rooms and then being expected to pay through the nose for them. Timeshares are particularly notorious as a scam-infested business, but they are by no means the only type of accommodation where tourists can be swindled. Unscrupulous hotel managers and even fellow guests all find travellers easy targets.

Tourist authorities are aware of the damage these scams do to their country's or city's image. They do their best to shut the criminals down but as soon as they close down one scammer, another springs up.

1. Hotel tout scams

Likely damage: 1/5

Frequency: 4/5

Countries reported: Global, mostly poor countries

Summary: Pushy touts meet travellers off planes or buses and use a variety of tactics to sell them rooms for the night.

Anyone who has travelled at all in poorer countries will be familiar with the following scene, which is repeated in hundreds of towns and cities in dozens of countries, often several times per day. It runs as follows.

A bus or train filled with tourists arrives. The doors open, and the travellers try to retrieve their cases and gather their bearings.

They are immediately besieged by touts who shove flyers advertising hotels or tours into their hands.

The touts demand, with varying degrees of urgency and persistence that the new arrivals use the services which they advertise. The touts completely ignore the locals on the bus, but swarm around the tourists like locusts in a cornfield.

The more persistent of the touts will grab a traveller's bags and take them to a waiting taxi, leaving the traveller virtually no choice but to go with them, or cause a scene by refusing, demanding the bags back and if necessary calling the police.

Even if they do not resort to this extreme tactic, however, touts will often make wildly misleading claims about the qualities of the hotel they are trying to sell. If business is slow, competition for the few arrivals can even lead to fights between touts.

Almost every tout will be paid a commission by their hotels for each guest they drag back, which is then added to the guest's bill at the end of their stay. In many tourist towns, there are usually far too many hotel rooms, meaning that hotels have to resort to these desperate tactics to break even, and this desperation rubs off on the touts. They may well only be able to eat tomorrow if they manage to persuade you to choose their hotel.

These touts are despised everywhere. In Tanzania, for instance, the locals nickname them *papasi*, a Swahili word meaning ticks or lice. A traveller can make use of them if he has arrived in a town without booking anywhere to stay, but it is important not to trust them. Let's offer a crumb of consolation, though – the touts will ensure that a traveller at least has a roof over his head for his first night. And if the tourist has the time, patience and bargaining skills, he can often haggle them down to a reasonable price for the room, though it will usually be higher than he could pay had he booked online or over the phone.

While using touts, however, it is helpful to bear in mind what they actually want. They want to get their target to the hotel which will give them commission. Once there, the traveller will be much less likely to go somewhere else, particularly if he has arrived late in the evening, or if the hotel is away from other accommodation in the town. The touts are therefore motivated to lie about the merits of the hotel they are recommending. They may say that it has a swimming pool, or that the rooms are air-conditioned, when neither is the case, and they are likely to offer the traveller rooms at a lower price than the traveller ends up paying when he gets to the hotel.

For travellers who do not want to deal with touts, there are a number of options for getting rid of them. If the traveller has a reservation at another hotel, or even if she does not, she can tell the touts that she does. This gets rid of most of them, but surprisingly others will still urge her to go with them. Some of the touts will tell the most extraordinary lies to persuade her to agree to stay at their hotel. My personal favourites (which I have actually heard) are that:

- The hotel has a problem with bedbugs

- It has closed

- It has burned down in a fire!

It can be surprisingly hard to ignore the hotel touts who are so desperate for business. Most of us are brought up not to ignore people who catch our eye or attempt to talk to us. It therefore seems wrong simply to say nothing and to walk determinedly away, though this usually gets rid of all but the most persistent touts eventually. To get rid of hotel touts, I have learned two useful tricks:

1. I say that I have booked a room on a reputable and well-known website such as Hotels.com or Hostelworld.com. This will make even the most desperate tout realise that I have a reservation to which I intend to stick.

2. I pretend that I do not speak either English or the local language. I become a Russian, Spaniard or Dane! Again, all but the most persistent touts will turn their attention to other targets, if they think that I will not understand them.

Virtually all the touts offering travellers hotel rooms when they arrive in a city are locals looking for tourists to choose the accommodation which they are selling. The damage which almost everybody will suffer from this scam is therefore fairly low, compared to many of the others detailed in this book. The worst problem a traveller will have is a couple of nights in unsuitable or overpriced accommodation. Occasionally, however, the touts' motives for getting tourists into their cars or taxis are more sinister. There have been reports of travellers met by hotel touts being lured into the back of taxis, then taken to the back streets of the city, and being mugged and, if female, raped as well. This is mercifully rare around the world, but it is common enough in some countries (for example Bolivia) that their governments warn tourists against it.

2. Half-built hotel scam

Likely damage: 2/5

Frequency: 2/5

Countries reported: Global.

Summary: Hotels and cruise ships where construction is proceeding while tourists are staying.

In the 1970's, mass tourism was just beginning in Europe and North America, pouring unimaginable amounts of money into previously sleepy towns and villages. Many towns wanted their share. To accommodate the huge influx, however, they had to create a tourist industry more or less from scratch. This meant hiring thousands or tens of thousands of staff very quickly. It also meant building hotels, roads, restaurants, airports and so on, on empty beaches or fields.

The city of Cancun was typical of this huge boom. In 1970, the government of Mexico decided to build a tourist town on a part of its coast where, previously, there had only been a few scattered settlements. A rumour has it that the site was chosen by a computer; however it was picked, they certainly chose well. The beaches around the city in the *zona hotelera* are white and powdery and the water is warm and inviting.

Within four years, the city was well on its way to being the most popular tourist destination in southern Mexico. A similar, breakneck, pace of development was happening on the Costa del Sol in Spain at the same time.

They built so fast, however, that a number of teething troubles affected the new industry, and ruined, or at least seriously damaged, the holidays of a large number of guests. Most were traceable to the teething troubles of a new industry, but a number of practices by hotels and other parts of the industry were so dishonest that they deserve to be called scams. One particular rip-off about which tourists complained was that they were sold rooms in hotels which were not yet completed. When the building works fell behind schedule, as building works all over the world often do, the tourists would sometimes find themselves without a place to stay. If they did have a room in a finished part of the hotel, work would still be continuing on the unfinished part, meaning loud noise in the early morning. Plumbing was often woefully inadequate. Swimming pools did not exist at all. Photographs of the hotel in the glossy travel agents' brochures bore no relation to the reality.

Many tourists complained about being misled and ripped off in this way. In those early days, mechanisms for complaints and refunds were non-existent. The unlucky tourists could often do little more than feel aggrieved, and warn their friends when they got home. This scam was in fact so common at the time that a successful English film, the comedy *Carry on Abroad* (1972), had a plot which revolved around the problems of a group of English package tourists arriving at a half-built hotel in Spain.

Amazingly, 40 years after mass tourism began, resorts are *still* selling tourists rooms in unfinished hotels or hotels under renovation, where construction is proceeding. This has recently been reported from the United States, Thailand, Spain, Turkey, Poland and Vietnam, amongst other countries, but it appears to be widespread enough to be called global.

There are various measures to reduce the likelihood of falling victim to this particular scam:

Before reserving a room in a hotel, it is best to choose one with good reviews online over the past two or three years. This should mean that, at least, you will not have to stay in a hotel which is being built around you. In turn, check the latest reviews carefully – if building works are taking place now (and affecting people's holidays) someone is very likely to flag it up.

It is even possible to check the hotel out on Google Earth, to ensure that it is not in an area where lots of construction work is happening all the time. Of course, it is always possible for construction work to start anywhere at any time, so checking out the hotel in this way does not ensure that you will avoid this problem during your stay.

If you are worried that construction work is likely at the hotel at which you plan to stay, the next step should be to ask the manager of the hotel whether work is planned during your stay. Of course, the manager could talk down the likely impact of renovations, or could be unaware that work needs to take place while the tourist is there, but there is at least a good chance that if he plans major work, he will admit it.

If you are seriously concerned that work is taking place, but you have to stay at that hotel for some reason, it might be a good idea to get any denials in writing or over e-mail. While this will do nothing to ensure a quieter holiday, it will make complaining to a tourist authority later, easier.

Tourists booked into "5-star" Greek hotel still being built

In 2015, a number of British holidaymakers were booked into a Greek hotel which was still being built. According to the *Daily Mail*, tourists who had spent hundreds or thousands of pounds on their holidays arrived to find construction still going on. Tourists had to mix with construction workers, and there were building materials everywhere. Many posted on Twitter or TripAdvisor to warn other travellers. One said, "Our room had a broken toilet flush that either didn't work or overflowed continually even though a plumber visited 3 times".

Eventually, the tour company moved most customers and offered them partial refunds.

3. Resort fees and other hotel "bait and switch" scams

Likely damage: 3/5

Frequency: 2/5

Countries reported: Global.

Summary: Hotels load extra charges onto their customers and give them worse rooms than they booked.

Resort fees are classic hidden charges which hotels often use, especially in the United States, to pad their profits. They are perfectly legal but rarely advertised as part of the price of booking the room, though, in fact, no customer can avoid paying them once he or she has stayed at the hotel. Hotels often pretend that these fees are in exchange for services like access to a gym, high-speed Internet or Cable TV in their rooms and are not room rates, so that they do not have to be disclosed before the room is booked. In fact, even if the resort fee is supposed to be in exchange for pool and a gym use, and even if the pool and the gym are both closed for the duration of the traveller's stay, the hotel will not refund it!

The mandatory resort fee scam, however, is only one of a family of tricks which are essentially "bait and switch" scams: the hotel tempts the traveller with a lower price than he will end up paying, or with higher quality goods than he will be supplied with. "Bait and switch" ("B&S") is common in countries where weak law enforcement means that it is difficult to demand what you think you have paid for. I have been a victim of it in Bolivia and the Spanish Canary Islands. "B&S" is extremely simple, but can still ruin somebody's holiday easily enough. It has many variants, but runs roughly as follows:

1. A customer books a specific hotel or apartment, either on its own or as part of a package. He is led to believe that he has booked high-quality accommodation in a good location. He books the rest of his trip accordingly.

2. At the last minute, however, he is rung up by the company with whom he booked his accommodation. He is told that the room or house is not available all of a sudden. Would the customer mind renting a different room or house, but in a "similar" place?

3. If the customer does not want to miss out on the rest of his trip, and cannot face finding accommodation again at such short notice, he will probably agree. The scammer may even offer a small refund if the customer complains enough.

4. When the customer arrives at the property, he finds that it is much cheaper and nastier accommodation than he has been led to expect.

5. If the customer insists on having something at a similar standard, the scammer will charge him much more than he agreed to pay previously.

6. Again, the customer may calculate that finding cheaper, better quality accommodation would be too much of a hassle, so he may let himself be swindled.

In fact, the customer probably never stood any chance of staying in the original property. It may not exist, it may be damaged, or the company he is dealing with may simply have received a better offer for it after the victim had booked. In any case, this amounts to a swindle, and is illegal in many countries. The scammers have obtained the victim's money under false pretences, luring him with promises of quality which they never intended to fulfil.

The best way to avoid this scam is to research hotels or beach houses thoroughly before paying any money, either as a deposit or as full payment for the room or rental property. In addition:

- Check online to see if the hotel has a reputation for "bait and switch" behaviour, or other unethical practices. Bear in mind that if it has just opened, or previously traded under a different name, you may have difficulty finding it.

- If you are going to a hotel that you suspect may charge "resort fees" or similar mandatory extra charges, call the hotel (rather than the booking company) and make sure that you are told, in writing if possible, exactly what you will be paying each day.

- Other "bait and switch" scams are most likely to occur when room availability is tight, because your accommodation is more likely to have other, more attractive offers, and you are less likely to be able to find another place to stay easily. If you are travelling at busy times, and have reason to believe that your hotel or resort may try and scam you in this way, get as much confirmed in writing as possible.

- Do not hesitate to complain to the tourist police, if there are any, and post your experiences online if your fears are realised. Sometimes, making a noise may not help you get your money back but it will at least warn other travellers about the hotel.

Examples of resort fees

Resort fees are often charged at hotels in Las Vegas. A helpful list on the website vegas.com shows that resort fees are currently charged by a number of hotels including some of the famous casinos. They currently range from $1/night to $25/night. That room you thought you were getting for $60/£50 per night can therefore cost you up to $85/£70 per night. To add insult to injury, you are often required to pay state sales or hotel tax on top of the resort fee, bumping the bill up even further.

These fees are not confined to Las Vegas; hotels in other American and Canadian cities seem to be seizing the opportunity to charge their customers in this way. One of the leading hotels in Banff, British Columbia charges a resort fee of C$5.25/night. On Maui, I have come across two hotels that charge a $25/night resort fee. More and more hotels charge these fees, meaning that it is important to check before you book.

4. Travel website or guidebook-related scams

Likely damage: 2/5

Frequency: 2/5

Countries reported: Global, especially in North Africa, Latin America and South and South-East Asia.

Summary: How guidebook-recommended hotels and other accommodation can deteriorate, and why hotels with similar names spring up.

Websites such as TripAdvisor.com or Yelp.com, which crowd-source reviews of accommodation, restaurants and other attractions, have become more and more important to many travellers in recent years. Online, customer-generated ratings also have a direct impact on what a hotel or restaurant can charge. A good review or two can make a hotel, while a couple of bad opinions can ruin it. A 2011 Harvard Business School study found that when restaurants increased their ranking by one star on leading customer review site Yelp, revenue increased between five and nine per cent. A Cornell University study determined that increasing review scores by one point (on a five point scale) allowed hotels to increase prices 11.2 per cent and still maintain occupancy levels.

Like the guidebooks still used by many tourists, travel websites usually recommend and review hotels in the country or city which they cover. Many hotels which have been reviewed well in a guidebook have a sticker displaying the guidebook's opinion of their business. A good review in a Lonely Planet or Let's Go is particularly important to hotels at the budget end of the price spectrum in poorer countries, as many backpackers will decide which hotel to go to on the basis of those reviews.

Unscrupulous hotels, however, can take advantage of tourists' reliance on reviews in guidebooks or on travel websites in a number of ways. They can use good reviews of different hotels to boost their business. They can find a hotel which has been well reviewed in a Lonely Planet or a Let's Go which covers their city. They then set up a hotel with a similar name, and send touts to the train station or airport to lure in travellers. They will claim that their hotel is the one that has been well-reviewed, hoping that some travellers will believe them.

Hotel managers also often take advantage of good reviews. Once a hotel has been well-reviewed, it may let its standards slip, particularly if it is full, or nearly so. No matter what the hotel's facilities are actually like, tourists will book in advance because of the good feedback. It is easier for hotels in the middle of nowhere to trick travellers in this way, where travellers cannot simply change their mind when they have seen the hotel with their own eyes.

Unscrupulous hotels or restaurants have also been known to bribe writers in exchange for favourable reviews. Many guidebook companies, such as Lonely Planet or Rough Guides, have long-standing policies that their reviewers should not accept free hospitality or gifts in exchange for good reviews, and no doubt almost all of their staff stick to these guidelines. The fact that they have to have these policies, however, suggests that reviewers could have been influenced by gifts; guidebook writers will probably be as open as anyone else to being bribed.

It seems as if every tourist has a different opinion on whether to use guidebooks or travel websites, and how seriously to take their opinions. For every traveller you meet who tells you that he has found a number of great hotels because his guidebook recommended them, there is another who has had his or her trip ruined by getting food poisoning at a recommended restaurant, and wishes not to have bought the guidebook at all. My own opinion is that reviews can often give very good advice. In using them for restaurants or hotel recommendations, however, it is important to bear in mind that:

- Individual reviews are only ever the reviewer's personal opinion on whatever they are describing. *Your* opinion may well differ, because of different tastes or for many other reasons. Two intelligent people can always have different, but perfectly valid, opinions on the same hotel/restaurant/tourist attraction and so on.

- Reviews are often out of date by the time they are published, let alone years later when they are still in use. The attractions which guidebooks describe in some countries, such as Western Europe or the United States may not change that much in that time, but other countries, such as China or Vietnam, are changing so fast that a five-year-old guidebook can easily be worthless.

- Once a popular guidebook or travel website features a destination which it claims is "off the beaten track", do not be surprised if the track is much more beaten than it used to be, by the time you get there. Lonely Planet guidebooks, in particular, have this effect in India and South America, and TripAdvisor can do so anywhere.

- Crowd-sourced websites, almost by definition, provide feedback from travellers to correct errors, or report changes. What is less often appreciated is that guidebooks do too. For this reason, if a guidebook is the first edition, I treat its comments and recommendations with a whole bucketful of salt, because it will not have had the feedback from travellers that later editions will have had.

TripAdvisor reviews scams

There are many articles documenting how fake hotel and restaurant reviews are written and published. The New York Attorney General investigated the practice in 2013, and the UK Competition and Markets Authority launched its own probe in 2013. In October 2015, the UK's *Daily Mail* reported that its correspondent had published an advertisement online, asking for good reviews of a fictitious Scottish restaurant, and had received 20 replies within an hour!

Short reviews that simply say how brilliant a place is, or a batch of reviews for a hotel/venue that seem to be written in a very similar way should raise suspicion. It is often worth looking at a reviewer's *other* reviews (you can do this by clicking on their username) to see whether they are serial *5-star-everything-is-great reviewers*. If they are, it is worth questioning why they are reviewing that particular hotel/venue, and whether the review is genuine.

5. Timeshare sales scams

Likely damage: 4/5

Frequency: 3/5

Countries reported: Most complaints seem to originate in Florida, Mexico and Southern Europe, particularly Spain.

Summary: Timeshare sales companies have a terrible reputation for scams. Many of them deserve it.

Timeshares are a cheap way for people to enjoy some of the benefits of having a second home. Rather than buying an apartment or house abroad, they buy the right to use it for a certain amount of time each year. They may or may not have a share in the ownership of the property but usually have to pay maintenance fees, including local property taxes. Many people who want to visit the same place each year have found this a convenient, and cheap, way to travel.

Many other timeshare owners, however, have found that they have paid over the odds for rights to use properties which are nothing like what they were sold. Many of the companies which sell timeshares have used questionable, and even fraudulent, sales tactics to the extent that a "timeshare sales pitch" is often code for a "scam".

Regulators have realised that the industry is swimming with sharks. The US Federal Trade Commission's Bureau of Consumer

Protection website, for example, publishes a five-page guide on how to avoid timeshare scams, and provides information on how to make a complaint. In 1994, the European Union passed a Directive aimed at stopping fraud in the sale of timeshares. The British Office of Fair Trading (OFT) launched a "crackdown" on shady timeshare sales practices in 2002 and again in 2007. All this regulatory activity, however, has not stopped all the scams in the industry, and plenty of complaints are still made each year. As soon as one scam is explicitly outlawed, or made very difficult, the companies move on to another swindle.

There are a number of common scams which companies or their agents use to sell their timeshares. In one of the newer tricks, the timeshare company promises that, if the customer is not satisfied with the property, the timeshare company will rent it out and guarantee the customer an extremely favourable return. It works like this:

1. A timeshare bought for say $25,000/£20,000 may come with a guarantee from the seller that it can be rented out at $2,500/£2,000 per year, a return of 10%. Given the current, low interest rates, this seems like a good return.

2. Investors hand over their money.

3. The company will then simply disappear after a year or two, leaving its customers without any guaranteed return on their money at all.

Timeshare touts often lure victims to a presentation with generous promises of free gifts. The presentations often last for hours, the free gifts usually fail to live up to the promises of the company, and occasionally the companies exert some mental (even physical) intimidation to force customers to stay when they want to leave and then sign them up. Some fraudulent timeshare companies attempt to lend their scams credibility by, for example, sending their customers official-looking documents from lawyers or government organisations. The documents are often forgeries and the government organisations frequently do not exist. They may have stamps which are designed to look as if they come from an industry association, which will also turn out not to exist.

Of course, the timeshare business is sales-driven and even some of the more legitimate agents may try to pressure a victim to buy a timeshare by touting a higher than normal fee which gets 'reduced' by 50% if the purchase signs up that day. In a neat switch, the agent may subsequently say that their manager has pulled rank and refused the reduction, but that they might be able to let them have 50% off once the property has been sold. Guess what? The reduction never materializes once the sale has been completed. This is a tactic often used by telesales business to hurry customers into a sale.

Some timeshare schemes are great and have many happy customers but here are a number of steps to take before entering into any deal.

Consider your timeshare as a place where you will stay on vacation, not just this year or next year, but over the next decade or so. Your needs and those of your family may change as the years pass. It is unwise to consider a timeshare as an investment property.

It is extremely unwise to sign a contract without understanding it. If necessary, hire a lawyer to review the contract, though fraudulent timeshare companies are often very slick at what they do and even experienced lawyers may not catch all their tricks.

Obvious danger signals are high-pressure sales tactics and offers of free gifts if customers agree to sign on the spot. Good deals sell themselves: they do not usually need somebody pressuring customers to sign while telling them what a great deal it is.

Companies that try to pressure their customers into signing without a lengthy cooling-off period are often acting illegally.

Customers should be sure that they know what they are buying. It is best to *visit* a timeshare before buying it, looking for signs of good property management.

Without an absolutely cast-iron guarantee to the contrary, and even then, bear in mind that management fees can change, usually only upwards. If the timeshare is abroad, the buyer will most likely be paying those fees in foreign currency, so bear in mind that changes in the exchange rate can cause them to increase, even if they are guaranteed in the local currency.

UK timeshare fraud gang smashed by Spanish police

In 2015, Spanish police arrested 56 people, all British, for timeshare fraud. The gang had been operating for seven years against hundreds, possibly thousands, of victims on the Costa del Sol. The scammers would trick the (mostly British) victims into surrendering their timeshares, then pose as lawyers and court officials to dupe them into handing over more money. Eleven companies were set up to perpetrate the fraud, and the proceeds were laundered in offshore bank accounts.

Las Vegas timeshare scam group charged

In January 2016, six people were charged with 11 counts of fraud. Their victims each lost thousands of dollars and were unaware they had fallen victim to a scam until they received bills from their respective timeshare companies for yearly fees. The accused allegedly operated World Travel Access, also known as Travel Solutions, Travel Solutions LLC dba World Travel Access, and WTA Services LLC. Between August 2013 and July 2014, they told victims that they would transfer timeshare ownership in exchange for an upfront fee. However, they never "actually attempted to transfer ownership of a timeshare" or refunded any money, according to the indictment. The scammers started the ball rolling by inviting victims to a presentation about transferring timeshare ownership.

6. Accommodation rental scam

Likely damage: 3/5

Frequency: 2/5

Countries reported: Global.

Summary: Travellers who have booked accommodation online find that the hotel or apartment does not actually exist.

Most companies offering holiday accommodation for rent are genuine, but some are not. Some (see scams #1 and #2) overstate the merits of their hotel, but others offer rooms which do not exist at all. This scam is an old favourite; it is simple, and all too easy to fall for. It relies on the fact that most of us rarely see the vacation properties we rent before we arrive there.

One of its many variants runs as follows:

1. The scammer places an advertisement for a beautiful beach house or ski chalet at a very attractive price in a nice resort. It might be in a magazine or on the Internet, which is more and more popular with swindlers because of its anonymity. The advertisement will be very well-presented and expensive looking. It may even have several fake testimonials, apparently from previous clients. The advertisement persuades the victim (Alice) to rent the property.

2. Alice pays for the rental in advance, either wholly or in part.

3. Alice arrives at the airport and travels to where the beach house or ski chalet should be. There is no such place.

4. Bewildered, Alice tries to find it for several hours, showing photos around town if she has brought them, or the address if she

has not. Nobody has heard of it, however. Fuming, she rents a hotel room for the night, and calls the resort company, but their phone lines are disconnected.

5. The victim never hears from the company again, and certainly never gets her money back. If she paid by credit card, she may be covered by their fraud insurance, but otherwise she has been swindled out of a lot of money and put to considerable inconvenience.

Another similar scam involves renting out a property which *does* exist, but which does not belong to the people renting it out. Because of the increase in foreclosures in parts of the western United States after the property bust there around 2005-7, repossessed properties in Las Vegas and around the Grand Canyon were particular favourites for criminals to advertise as vacation homes for some years thereafter. However, this scam can occur anywhere.

- The criminals rent the property to Alice, aiming to make her pay the usual hundreds or thousands of dollars as a deposit. The crooks may offer to arrange a viewing AFTER Alice has handed over a deposit, though she will probably find that the viewing is mysteriously cancelled at the last minute.

- Alice will then turn up at the property, and find that somebody else is already using it.

- If it is empty, Alice may try to enter the property to see what is going on. If she is extremely unlucky, she may be arrested for breaking and entering.

- At best she will lose a lot of money, at worst she could have a stressful evening explaining her story to the police.

A fraud along these lines was committed at the ski resort of Verbier, Switzerland (see example, below). The cantonal police in

Valais, where Verbier is situated, recommend the following precautions to reduce the risk of falling victim to this scam while trying to rent property there:

- Tourists should research the rental company, reaching a contact person by other means than the internet or fax.

- Tourists should always call the tourism office to check that the accommodation exists and that there have been no complaints about it.

- It may also be worth contacting the beneficiary's bank, which should provide written information about the customer.

- It seems unwise to hand over any money at all without being sure that the accommodation exists and that it is what the company says it is.

- A tourist can always ask for the property's address and see if he can find it on Google Earth. If not, he or she should at least call the rental agency and raise the concerns with them, before parting with any money.

Another way to avoid many of these scams is to ask to view the property, BEFORE handing over any money as a deposit. Most of the time, the renter cannot do so, because he lives hundreds or thousands of miles away. Hopefully, the person he is talking with will not know this. If the person trying to rent the apartment does not own it, he will probably resist showing it to the tourist, and the tourist should be very suspicious if the person he is talking to will not let him see the property he plans to rent, at least from the outside.

Spanish villa website fraud

According to the Daily Mirror, in December 2016, a British family booked a villa in Spain through a website called luxurycanarianrentals.com. They paid £2,084/$2,600 in cash, which is never recommended. There was no transport to meet them at the airport, so they booked a taxi to the villa, and realised they had been scammed. Fortunately, they were able to find alternative accommodation, at considerable cost.

Another instance of this form of fraud, reported by the Daily Mail in 2017. Ten friends had paid more than £4,000/$5,000 through BACS to secure a villa in Ibiza which they had seen advertised online. However, the listing was fraudulent, and it seems they lost their money. As they paid through electronic transfer, rather than by credit card, it will be much more difficult for them to get their money back.

Increase in villa fraud, 2017

The UK police's National Fraud Intelligence Bureau (NFIB) warned the public against a large increase in fraudulent websites, which it estimated had increased 425% between 2015 and 2016! City of London police commander Chris Greany, national co-ordinator for economic crime, said: "When booking a holiday, it is vitally important you take your time and follow a number of basic checks designed to protect you from falling victim to a fraud. These include researching the name of the company online you are considering using and ensuring it is a member of a recognised trade body. It is also key that you make sure the website is legitimate by carefully checking the domain name and pay with a credit card, rather than using a debit card or cash." The police named two websites in particular, luxuryrentalsvilla.com and cycladesrentals.com, which it had shut down.

Anglo-Swiss chalet rental fraud

In 2008 and 2009, several wealthy tourists tried to rent Chalet Lumiere, which pretended to be a luxury, six-bedroom chalet in the centre of the Swiss ski resort of Verbier. It had a very slick website, skichalet-verbier.com, though there was no mailing address, only a British fax number, amongst the contact details. In December 2009, a British couple paid more than SFr 12,300 ($12,300/£10,000) per week to rent the chalet, and turned up in Verbier with their ski equipment, only to find that the chalet did not exist.

They were persuaded to lodge complaints with the police in Britain and Switzerland and were put up in a hotel at the tourist authority's expense. The office had already had several inquiries from concerned holiday makers who had paid deposits. The chalet's website has since been shut down. It was hosted in London but registered in Canada by a shell company, meaning that there was no way to trace it, or for victims to get their money back. Verbier has had several similar scams in the past few years, though they remain exceptional, and most people renting chalets to go skiing at the Swiss resort have a great time. It is a lovely town with great ski slopes.

7. Hotel exchange rate scam

Likely damage: 2/5

Frequency: 2/5

Countries reported: Global

Summary: Hotels rip travellers off with ruinous exchange rates, and then charge them ridiculous commissions when they pay their bills.

Hotels are always looking for ways to extract more money from their customers. The room rates are never enough, especially now, with falling occupancy rates and increasingly cost-conscious travellers. Ripping tourists off through charging outrageous prices for drinks from the minibar or the use of the phone in the tourist's room is virtually universal. There are three sneaky ways in which hotels make significant money from their customers in return for foreign currency.

One way to do so is to take advantage of international travellers' need to change money. Tourists may need cash for their travels, or to settle the hotel's bill at the end of the stay. Hotels often advertise that they do not charge commission for these transactions. However, when the tourist arrives back home weeks later and checks his bill, he finds that the hotel has, in fact, added a commission to the bill. As the victim will not get the bill until he is back home, probably in a different country, he will be unlikely to complain even if he notices the deceit.

But the money hotels get from scamming tourists in this way is apparently not enough, and they make further profit from the exchange rates which they advertise. They are very unfavourable to their customers, and favourable to the hotel. The hotel can change money at a bank at a much more favourable rate than it gives its customers. Tourists can even be better off going to the worst *bureau de change* in the city than changing money at their hotel. I was in Tel Aviv and saw an expensive hotel which offered to exchange dollars for Israeli shekels at 3.2 while the wholesale rate was 3.6 and most bureaux de change were offering 3.4 or 3.5. Changing $1,000 at a hotel, therefore, can easily cost you $100.

A third way in which hotels have been known to scam foreign tourists through unfavourable exchange rates is more underhand. It is known as Dynamic Currency Conversion (DCC). According to Visa, travellers in a foreign country paying for services using its cards should be offered the choice of paying in their home currency, or the currency where the transaction takes place. In practice, this rarely, if ever happens. What happens instead is that:

1. A hotel presents a bill to the tourist at the end of his stay. It is added up in local currency – say it comes to 10,000 Pesos, which

might equal $1,000 at the credit card company's exchange rate, or $1,100 at the hotel's exchange rate.

2. The tourist pays using his credit card, and thinks nothing more of it.

3. The hotel, without telling the tourist, charges him in his home currency at its unfavourable exchange rate.

4. When the tourist gets his credit card bill a few weeks later, however, the bill in his local currency is much higher than he thought it would be ($100 higher in the above example). He had thought that they were charging his credit card account in local currency and the credit card company would do the conversion at its favourable exchange rates.

5. The hotel can then change the foreign currency at a much more favourable rate than it has given the traveller: the 10,000 Peso bill comes to $1,100 rather than $1,000. The difference between the hotel's rate and the credit card company's rate is often 5-10% and can be higher.

Other businesses besides hotels use DCC, and charge tourists extra (undisclosed) commissions and fees for using their credit or debit cards. I prefer not to settle hotel bills or pay for restaurant meals using a credit card, unless there is no alternative. The danger of being ripped off by unscrupulous merchants who now have my credit card details is too great, and the insurance that credit card companies give on purchases is worthless, since I have already eaten the meal or stayed at the hotel. I cannot return the meal which I have eaten and ask for a refund. When possible, I prefer to withdraw money from an ATM and pay for meals or hotels in cash and in the local currency. At least that way, I know what I have paid and the hotel or restaurant has no way to charge me more.

A further cause of unexpectedly high charges on a credit card used abroad can be traced to the credit card company, rather than the hotel or restaurant. The credit card company may decide to levy a surcharge on the bill for paying abroad in the local currency (say, dollars). If the hotel had billed the credit card company in its currency (say, pesos), the credit card company would have been entitled to charge its customer a fee for converting his money from dollars to pesos. To make good on the loss of a fee, some credit card companies therefore charge a commission of 2-3% of the bill (often called the "International Service Charge") if their customers spend in their local currency overseas, even though the credit card company is not required to change the currency to pesos. So if the hotel charges its customer an unfavourable exchange rate which costs him 5%-10% extra for billing him in dollars and your credit card company charges him an extra 2-3% for doing nothing, he is being charged an extra 7-13%, which on a large hotel bill can be a lot of money.

Before using a credit or debit card extensively overseas, it can also be worth checking your credit card company's Schedule of Charges. Find out whether they charge an International Service Fee on transactions overseas, and the precise circumstances under which that fee applies. This allows you to make an informed decision about whether to use the card, or pay with cash, when paying for expensive purchases while travelling.

8. Online hotel booking site review scam

Likely damage: 3/5

Frequency: 3/5

Countries reported: Global.

Summary: Related to travel website or guidebook-related scams (#4), hotels and other businesses post reviews of their *own* businesses on other websites, but do not mention that the reviewer is connected with the hotel.

Many travellers now book their accommodation through websites such as TripAdvisor.com, Hotels.com or Fodor.com. Hotels can be found and compared very quickly on these and similar websites. The websites often allow customers of the hotels to post reviews, which can be very helpful to travellers who want to find out if a particular hotel is suitable for them or not. As the sites are free, and can make money if customers book hotels through them, they are driving many hotel guidebooks out of business.

However, owners of hotels and other forms of accommodation have quickly realised how important a good online review can be, in steering travellers to their businesses. The less scrupulous therefore post reviews online themselves, stating that their hotel offers wonderful value for money; has first class facilities; is very conveniently located for whatever attractions there are in the area; and has friendly and welcoming staff. They try to create the impression, and often say explicitly, that these reviews are written by travellers who have stayed with them. They do not declare their interest in the business.

Many websites also allow travellers to rate hotels by attributes such as location, facilities and value for money, usually on a percentage basis, or out of ten or five stars. If hotel staff can rate their hotels on a website, they can bump up their rating from one star to four stars very quickly, providing that there are not too many other reviews yet. Websites often try to screen out obviously fake reviews or ratings by having a member of their staff read them, or "moderate" them. As they will usually admit, however, they cannot screen out *every* bogus review.

Travellers reading hotel booking websites can be fooled by unfavourable reviews, as well as favourable reviews. If a hotel's owners or employees can go online and print false reviews, so can the owners or employees of its competitors. They can claim that their competitor is infested by bugs, or is badly located or has unfriendly staff, and they can move its ratings down from four-star to one-star very quickly.

Even genuine reviews are, at the end of the day, only one person's opinion. Different reviews will probably look for different features in a hotel (though of course liking low prices and disliking bedbugs are fairly universal!). To avoid being fooled by fake reviews:

- It is useful to read as many reviews online as possible, on two or three different websites, particularly for stays of many nights. Many fake reviews are relatively easy to spot.

- Even on sites with no reviews (just ranking values) sudden and dramatic changes in ratings over a few hours can be a sign that a hotelier is trying to bump his hotel up the rankings deliberately, or that the hotel is a victim of a campaign by competitors.

- Hotels owned by one person or a family are presumably more likely to try and fiddle reviews than big chains like Holiday Inns or Hiltons.

- Bear in mind that reviews on websites like TripAdvisor.com and Fodors.com are often dated, and if a hotel has been reviewed several times within a month or so, in nearly identical language, and if these reviews are contradicted by most of the other reviews of the hotel on the website, then they are highly likely to be fake. This is particularly likely if they express extreme opinions, either that the hotel was excellent, or that it was awful. Sometimes, however, the hotel's owner is shrewder, and the fake reviews can be close to indistinguishable from genuine comments.

Fake reviews on booking.com discovered

In 2017, The Telegraph reported that a guest of a hotel in Morocco had found that her ID on Booking.com had been used to leave a fake review. Booking.com only allows registered users to post reviews. However, the tourist had presented a copy of her booking confirmation when she checked in to the hotel. The hotel had then apparently used the PIN and reference number on the confirmation email to log in as the tourist and post a favourable review. Booking.com removed the review and announced a "full investigation" in cooperation with the hotel.

Chapter 2: Transport scams

Scammers realise that travellers are particularly vulnerable while they are using public transport or taxis. They have many, if not all, of their possessions with them, and are often tired and preoccupied. It is relatively difficult to target travellers in the heavily policed parts of airports, though many scammers pick on travellers as soon as they have passed through customs.

It is far easier to scam travellers when they are on trains and buses, and in train and bus stations however. Many countries and cities have realised this, and have introduced improved security, including CCTV on public buses, and uniformed guards at train and bus stations. But scammers still try to target tourists.

Taxi drivers as a group have a very bad reputation for scamming travellers (and locals) worldwide. Tourists often have little choice but to use taxis to get around foreign cities. Since they do not know the way themselves, and are often unfamiliar with local prices and customs, tourists make tempting targets for the unscrupulous. As taxi drivers are often self-employed, it is easier to find work despite criminal convictions, though of course *many are honest*.

A complete list of the ways in which taxi drivers routinely scam travellers would make this book as long as an encyclopaedia. More complaints must be made about taxi drivers than about any other profession involved in the tourism industry. Many governments of countries with big tourist industries are aware of this, and have tried to regulate and control taxi drivers and prevent their most fraudulent practices. Often, however, attempts to prevent scams have failed, and even if they have succeeded, taxi drivers have simply moved on to the next rip-off.

Licensed taxis are usually safer than unlicensed cabs. It is also more difficult for taxi drivers to scam their passengers if the passenger has some idea of where they are going, how to get there, and how much it should cost. Taxis which present themselves to a tourist should always be treated with more suspicion than those which you hail on the street. It is better to have some small banknotes or coins available to pay the fare as taxi drivers do not always have the correct change.

9. Taxi meter scams

Likely damage: 2/5

Frequency: 4/5

Countries reported: Global, particularly common in poorer countries.

Summary: Taxi drivers fiddle with their meters to charge their passengers more.

This family of scams is one of the most widespread of those covered in this book, but, though annoying, it is not usually particularly dangerous or damaging to its victims. In many countries, taxi drivers are required to install meters in their taxis. They must charge travellers, and locals who use their services, a fixed price at the start of the journey and another fixed price for each kilometre or mile travelled. These tariffs can vary, depending on the time of the ride, the number of people in the cab and whether or not they carry luggage. In addition, taxi drivers can sometimes charge more if they leave the centre of a city. These regulations are designed to protect the customers of the taxi drivers, who can be reasonably sure that they will not be charged excessive amounts for their journeys if the system works as it should.

Unfortunately, there are many possibilities for fraud.

One of the most common ways for taxi drivers to demand more money than they are entitled to, is simply to break the meter. Taxi drivers in poorer countries will often only announce that the meter is broken at the end of a journey, and take the risk that the tourist will refuse to pay, though they may tell the tourist that the meter is broken at the start of the journey, and demand a higher price for the fare. The tourist will of course be unfamiliar with taxi regulations in the foreign city, and unaware that the taxi driver has just violated said regulations. Most tourists will therefore pay, especially if they do not yet understand the local currency. A few will not, but the taxi driver may intimidate them, or may demand a lower fare. The taxi driver may even simply write the fare off, especially if the passenger threatens to call the police.

Even if the taxi driver lets his meter run, he can still manipulate it in any number of ways. One of the most common scams, and one of the most difficult to spot, is when the taxi driver simply changes the settings on the meter, so that it shows the night-time fare for day-time journeys. As the night-time fare is commonly half as high again (and can be twice as high as the day-time fare) this means that the customer will pay much more than they should. Often, the meter will show a number which indicates whether the day-time or the night-time fare is being charged, but the passenger will not know that a different fare is charged at night, or how to spot the settings on the meter. In the unlikely event that the passenger does notice and insist that the meter be changed, the taxi driver can of course simply apologise and comply. He will have lost nothing at all through being detected in his dishonesty – he will still receive the normal, legal fare. This scam is therefore extremely low risk for the taxi driver, though it is probably slightly higher-risk if he tries it on a local, who would be more aware of how much a journey should cost.

The taxi driver can often change the rate at which the meter runs by fiddling with the meter itself, so that, instead of charging a fixed sum per kilometre, it will charge the same fixed sum per five hundred meters. Again, it is unlikely that the traveller will spot this scam. Only an occasional inspection of the meter by the city authorities would spot what the taxi driver had been up to.

Taxi-drivers may even have reasonable, or semi-reasonable, excuses for treating travellers and locals in this way. Often, the government may have set the fares so low that the taxi-driver cannot cover his costs and make an honest living if he plays by the rules. This is particularly likely to be the case in very poor countries if the price of oil has risen significantly recently: governments often move slowly to increase regulated taxi fares, if they do so at all, and a big increase in the price of fuel can mean that taxi drivers actually lose money carrying passengers if they play by the rules. This was the case in Amman, Jordan: taxi-drivers simply refused to carry travellers if they insisted that the taxi driver switch on the meter!

Most travellers are ripped off by taxi drivers at some point in their travels. Precautions which you can take include:

- If the meter seems to be broken, or if it is off and the taxi driver refuses to turn it on, you should always attempt to negotiate a fare before getting into the taxi.

- If the taxi driver refuses to agree a fare, or insists on an unreasonable tariff, you should try and find another cab, unless of course there is unlikely to be one available.

- If you suspect that the meter has been tampered with, or that you are being charged a higher rate than should be the case, you can threaten to call the police, and actually do so. Many tourist centres have specialist, English-speaking tourist police. You will need the licence plate number of the taxi, and if possible the name of the taxi driver, to make a complaint.

- It is therefore helpful to be aware of how much a taxi ride from the airport should cost. Any good, reasonably up-to-date guidebook should contain this information. So should the web. Travellers are usually at their most vulnerable when they have just arrived in a city, and are on their way from the airport or train or bus station to their final destination, usually a hotel. So much is unfamiliar, often including the country's money, and unscrupulous taxi drivers are of course aware of this.

I am fairly sure that I have been cheated by taxi drivers in Ecuador, Thailand, China and Bosnia. I *know* I have been cheated in Istanbul (see example below). I have probably been ripped off in similar ways many times without realising it. Paying a few more dollars for a taxi ride may not be the worst experience a traveller will have on his or her trip, but this does not prevent it from being annoying!

My experience of being swindled by a taxi driver in Istanbul

I flew into Istanbul late one evening, and took a train from the airport to the tram station which would take me to where I needed to go. The tram had stopped for the night, so I decided to share a taxi with two Scottish tourists who were staying near where I was. We hailed a taxi which took us to where we wanted to go. When it came to paying, however, the taxi driver showed me the meter, which demanded 28,000,000 old Turkish lira (28 new Turkish lira, at the time worth $19/£12). In fact, the first "2" was the number of the tariff, which was at night, and had nothing to do with the fare, so we only owed the driver 8,000,000 old Turkish lira (8 new Turkish lira ($5/£3)). His swindling did not end there, however. I gave him a 50 lira note, which he replaced when I was not looking with a 5 lira note, and he pretended that I still owed him 23 lira. It was not the most pleasant introduction to Istanbul!

10. Robberies and gassings on overnight trains

Likely damage: 4/5

Frequency: 1/5

Countries reported: Italy, Eastern Europe, Thailand.

Summary: Travellers sleeping in compartments on overnight trains are gassed and their possessions are stolen.

Eurail (aka EuroRail) and InterRail passes entitle the traveller to travel on European trains for free (or at least cheaply). I and many others have made full use of the flexibility which such passes offer, and have really enjoyed every trip I have taken. Most users of these passes will at some time use one of the trains which cross Europe at night to get from one city to another, eight or ten hours away. They are particularly popular with young travellers on low budgets, since they can save the cost of a hotel room by sleeping on the train.

Most overnight trains in Europe are divided into compartments with benches which are used as three seats during the day, but which can also be used for beds at night. I myself have slept in a large number of these compartments in Europe, and also in South East Asia and Morocco. While far from luxurious, they are tolerable for a few hours.

The doors to the compartments can be closed and often locked. Each compartment opens on to a corridor which runs down the carriage, and to which anybody on the train has access.

Sleeping travellers on public transport are very vulnerable to anybody with an eye on their property and no scruples. A scam which has been reported on trains in Eastern Europe, Thailand and Italy, runs as follows:

1. The criminal (or criminals) open the door slightly and feed a tube attached to a cylinder of anaesthetic gas into the compartment.

2. They turn the gas on, knocking the travellers out.

3. They open the compartment door and rob their victims of whatever they are carrying.

4. The victims will wake up a few hours later, with headaches but unusually otherwise unharmed. They will notice that their valuables are gone, but without the slightest idea of what happened to them.

This scam has also been used by criminal gangs on the drivers of Heavy Goods Vehicles/Trucks. Many large trucks have sleeping quarters in the cabs for their drivers, and when the driver tucks in for the night, the gas is piped in, and the driver knocked out. When he wakes up – his load is gone.

Of course, as the scammers are not expert anaesthetists, they could overdo the dose of the gas, seriously injuring or even killing their victims. If their victims happen to be allergic to the gas, they could also be killed, even if the dosage is right for a normal person. Back on the train, criminals are unlikely to be disturbed committing their robbery, since most of the people on the train will be asleep at three or four o'clock in the morning. Any noise which they make will most likely be drowned out by the noise of the train. They may have bribed the guard or conductor on the train to see nothing. That same conductor, who will have been into every compartment collecting tickets, may even have helped the scammers by telling them which compartments are likely to have the best opportunities.

There is no need to be paranoid about this scam since the overwhelming majority of overnight journeys on trains are trouble free and this is a pretty rare scam overall. There are, however, a number of ways to make it less likely that you will be robbed while asleep in a train compartment:

- If a catch or other fastening is available, make sure that you use it to secure the door as much as possible. Remember, however, that these catches are designed for privacy rather than security, and thieves can usually force them open slightly with a minimum of effort.

- If there are any cracks between the door and the frame or the floor, through which somebody's hand, or a rubber tube, could conceivably be forced, block them using a suitcase or a backpack.

- Putting valuables in suitcases or backpacks and locking those cases closed, and then locking them to the benches or bolted-down tables in the train compartment, will prevent most casual thefts. The keys to those locks should not be left in plain view during the night. You should put them in your pocket, or otherwise out of sight. But remember, locks do not give total security, because the thieves may have knives or bolt cutters which will enable them to cut the straps of your backpack or force your case open.

- Any extra precautions you take, however, make it less likely that thieves will take the risk of trying to steal your property. It's a good rule of thumb that if you make life difficult for the villains the overall risks for them increase and they may figure things are 'not worth it'. It is also more likely that, if they do try to rob you, you will notice what is going on and be able to challenge them – whether you should do so or not, is another matter.

- To make it harder for anybody to knock you out using sleeping gas, sleep with your head as far away as possible from the door. In some overnight trains, air conditioning means that windows cannot be opened. If the window can be opened and it is warm enough outside to avoid freezing overnight, and if the noise from the train is not too much of a problem, it might be an idea to sleep with the window open, to prevent gas accumulating in the compartment in sufficient amounts to cause unconsciousness.

- If you are in a large party, or if one of you has difficulty sleeping on trains, at least one person at a time could stay awake, to make sure everybody else is safe. Obviously this may be deemed unnecessary on certain routes, but it is worth considering if you are passing through a country which is notorious for robberies on sleeping travellers. This precaution is probably excessive in most countries, however, given the rarity of this scam.

Robbery on an overnight train in the Alps

When travelling from Munich to Venice overnight in 1997 with a couple of friends, I very foolishly left my wallet with £100/$125 of cash in it on the floor of the compartment. We used the catch to fasten the door, and settled down for a good night's sleep. When I woke up, my wallet was empty of cash, though fortunately the ATM and credit cards in it were intact. Somebody must have forced the door open silently, taken the cash from my wallet, and then disappeared into the night. I have no reason to think that I was gassed, however! I have heard many similar stories from people who have travelled on overnight trains in Europe over the years.

Possible robbery of British couple in France, 2014

Any enclosed space can be used for gassing, if the victims are asleep or otherwise unaware of what is happening. A British couple were driving their campervan around France in 2014, and stopped for the night and went to sleep. When they awoke, they found several hundred pounds of valuables and their passports had been stolen. They considered that they were probably gassed, since they were both light sleepers. The French police had reported a number of similar robberies in the area.

However, there was no positive proof that chemical agents were used in the robbery, and it is worth noting that some experts were sceptical that thieves would have the necessary expertise and equipment to render their victims unconscious by using gas. Indeed, the Royal College of Anaesthetists believed it would be impossible. It issued a statement saying: "Even the more powerful modern volatile agents would need to be delivered in tankerloads of carrier gas by a large compressor".

11. Spiked drinks on public transport

Likely damage: 4/5

Frequency: 2/5

Countries reported: India, Pakistan, Thailand, Turkey, the Philippines, South America.

Summary: A traveller on a train or bus is befriended by a man who offers him a drugged drink. The traveller is robbed and may be sexually assaulted.

This scam is a combination of scam #10, in which tourists are gassed on overnight trains, and scam #38, in which tourists are drugged in bars. It is so often reported, and so horrifying, that it deserves a section of its own in this book. It is a clever way of rendering travellers unconscious, so that they can be robbed, or worse. It has been reported, in particular, from travellers on Indian railways, though I have also heard of it happening on Pakistani and Bolivian buses, and on trains in Thailand. Travelling by train is the classic way to get around India, and it is an experience in itself that is recommended.

Foreigners are invariably an object of curiosity, and Indians are by nature very friendly and inquisitive. They will often offer a traveller some of their food and drink, and may be slightly offended if the traveller refuses.

Traditions of hospitality, unfortunately, can be abused by criminals. Scammers pervert the practice of offering food or drink to strangers to drug their victims.

Most parents advise their children not to accept food or drink from strangers, however charming they may seem, and this advice still applies to grown-ups. Several drugs are used by scammers, and some of them, if used in heavy doses, can cause permanent harm to the victims, or even death. Rohypnol, scopolamine, Nembutal and benzodiazepine have all been used to drug travellers. By far the most common advice given to travellers is: *do not take food or drink from people you have just met.* The UK Foreign Office and the Indian police have both warned travellers to India about this crime. The Foreign Office, for example, advises British tourists on Indian railways: "Do not accept food or drinks from strangers. There have been reports of travellers being drugged and robbed on trains, more often than not on the overnight trains. Take particular care of your passport and valuables when boarding and whilst on the train".

It is unrealistic to expect everybody to follow this advice in all circumstances, particularly since it would mean refusing many generous and genuine offers of hospitality and causing offence in some cultures. The most realistic advice, therefore, is:

- Be extremely cautious before accepting food or drink from strangers.

- Do so only if you are sure that the strangers mean you no harm, and where there are lots of other people about.

- Be aware that, however friendly they may seem, your new acquaintances could be casting longing eyes at you and your possessions.

Two Indians arrested for drugging and robbing a Singaporean passenger

For much of the past decade, so-called "biscuit bandits" have been operating on India's rail network. These scammers feed drugged biscuits to victims, most of whom are Indian, not tourists.

In 2016, Indian police arrested two men who allegedly robbed a Singaporean national on a train. They claimed that the men had robbed many travellers by offering them dry fruits laced with sedatives, and that the men were part of a huge group operating in north India. On checking the luggage of the accused criminals, the police recovered Rs. 40,000 (£400/$500), six cell phones, and other valuables, including those belonging to the Singaporean national.

Police said the two men travelled on confirmed tickets and after befriending unsuspecting passengers, would offer them dry fruits laced with sedatives. Once their victims fell asleep, they would rob them. The police intended to make further efforts to catch the duo's accomplices.

Nine passengers robbed on Thai train

In 2014, passengers on a southbound train in Thailand were reportedly robbed in their sleep. Nine passengers said they lost their phones and cash in the theft. 30 passengers were in the car at the time. The perpetrator managed to remove sim cards from all the victims' phones and left them behind, in order to avoid tracking from the police.

One victim said that he and his companions were deep in their sleep when the theft happened, and only discovered that their belongings were missing when they woke up at 6 am. He also suspected that he and other victims may have been drugged by the perpetrator. Some were also dazed when they woke up.

12. Hijacking of tourist buses

Likely damage: 4/5

Frequency: 1/5

Countries reported: India, Guatemala, Peru, El Salvador.

Summary: Tourist buses are targeted for hijacking and robbery.

Tourist buses and minibuses are often a good way to travel, since they can be quicker and more comfortable than public buses. They usually deliver you directly to whatever sight you want to see. However, in many countries, tourist buses and minibuses are increasingly targets for local bandits. They are often easily distinguishable from public buses as they may well have the insignia of the travel agency painted on the side, and they are likely to have suitcases tied to the top.

Foreign tourists can be distinguished from natives through their skin colour, clothes and language. Thieves can, therefore, identify tourist buses relatively easily, hold them up and rob them.

Robberies from tourist buses (or boats, see the example below) are becoming more common in many countries, especially in South Asia and Latin America. While insurance will cover most of many victims' financial losses, the shock alone can easily ruin a holiday.

Robberies of tourist buses can occur anywhere, but by far the majority happen in certain areas of a very few countries. At the time of writing, Guatemala and India are the worst countries for this crime (see examples below). To minimise the risk that you will fall victim to this scam:

- Travellers in Central America, Africa or parts of South America and South Asia should be aware exactly where bandits are currently most active, by checking embassy websites and tourist websites such as LonelyPlanet.com and TripAdvisor.com.

- As hijackers prefer to strike on empty roads at night, travelling on busy highways during the day can reduce your chance of being robbed in this way.

It is worth bearing in mind that bandits target local buses, as well as tourist buses; even in Guatemala, tourist buses are targeted *less often* than local buses. Throughout Central America, local buses are frequently hijacked.

Separately, local bus companies in San Salvador, Guatemala City and Managua are often targeted by extortionists demanding that bus companies pay a form of 'protection money'. If they don't pay up, their buses (and the passengers) are sprayed with machine gun fire, or destroyed with grenades! At least with crime against tourist buses, the criminals only target tourists' property, rather than their lives.

Tourist bus hijacked and robbed in Mexico

In April 2017, a tourist bus with 25 Germans and three Mexicans was robbed as it was driving between San Cristobal de las Casas and the famous archaeological site of Palenque. The bus driver took a detour. Gunmen forced the bus to stop and boarded it, stealing cash and cameras from the tourists and their guides. The police reached the bus shortly after the robbers had escaped.

Tourist bus robbed in South Africa

A bus carrying tourists was robbed on the N4 at Pelindaba outside Pretoria, South Africa in April 2014. "It is alleged that three males driving a white Audi … shot at the bus carrying tourists, forcing it to stop," the police reported. "The suspects then entered the bus and demanded to be given all cell phones and handbags. The suspects then fled the scene. No one was injured".

13. Taxi mafia scams

Likely damage: 2/5

Frequency: 4/5

Countries reported: The Philippines, Thailand, Canada, India, Puerto Rico, Czech Republic, Estonia, France.

Summary: Taxi drivers cooperate with each other to fleece passengers.

In many tourist resorts or towns around the world, the taxi drivers charge high fares. The taxi mafia scam runs as follows:

1. The taxi drivers combine to form a mixture of a trade union and a cartel, designed to ensure that tourists have no choice but to use their services.

2. They often use intimidation or worse to make sure that no independent taxi drivers break their illegal monopolies.

3. They can then charge very high prices, whether or not the fares are regulated, especially if local police are weak and corrupt.

4. They often bribe the police to turn a blind eye to their activities. Sometimes, they have links with, or are part of, organised crime.

The prices that the taxi mafias charge are rarely enough to break any but the tightest budgets, but they can add up over a few weeks.

Thai beach resorts have a bad reputation for shady practices by taxi drivers, but they are by no means the only places where taxi mafias are to be found (see examples below). Many more examples can be found by reading tourist magazines or websites. It is probably true to say that tourist destinations from which taxi-related scams are *not* regularly reported are considerably rarer than countries from which they *are* regularly reported. Avoiding them is difficult, as my friend in the example below found in Thailand. You can, however, take some steps:

- In many cities, Uber, Lyft or other ride-sharing services provide welcome competition to taxi drivers. Often, however, pressure from taxi drivers have meant that bizarre restrictions are placed on their activities, and occasionally they are banned altogether.

- Where there is developed public transport, mastering the local bus or train routes can make avoiding overpriced taxi mafias relatively easy.

- Renting a car gives considerable flexibility, but exposes tourists to other scams (see scams #60 and #62).

- Hitchhiking is possible, but can be very dangerous in many countries, and is not recommended unless you have no choice.

- Demanding that the taxi-drivers charge a reasonable fare, and knowing the law, can sometimes get them to reduce their demands, but is as likely to annoy them, with unpredictable consequences.

Taxi mafia on Phuket, Thailand: one traveller's tale

A friend experienced this scam when travelling with his girlfriend on the island of Phuket. His experience seems to be typical of that of many budget travellers who have stayed on Phuket. He had been warned by other travellers that if he attempted to take a taxi from outside his hotel, the taxi driver was likely to try to rip him off. Bearing this warning in mind, he would walk out of his hotel, ignore the taxi rank there and attempt to hail taxis on the main road which ran to his favourite beach or to the nearby town. However, neither the island's taxis nor its many tuk-tuks would stop for him, so he was forced to go back to the hotel taxi rank and use them anyway.

Eventually, when my friend moved to another part of the island, he met a taxi driver who did not seem to be part of the taxi mafia. He was told that all independent taxi drivers on Phuket, and all tuk-tuk drivers, knew not to pick up tourists from his former hotel. The local taxi mafia wanted to keep their monopoly, and had bribed the local police accordingly. The management of the hotel saw its guests being ripped off every day, but were too afraid to do anything, and in any case it was the tourists, rather than the hotel, who were suffering from the scam. The Thai police have an extremely bad reputation for corruption, so, though local politicians occasionally criticised the taxi-drivers, nothing effective was ever done.

My friend (who is always up for a challenge) tried a number of ways to avoid dealing with the taxi mafia on Phuket:

- He would walk a mile or two down the main road which led to his beach, and attempt to hail a taxi. Evidently, however, a mile or more away from the hotel was not far enough for a foreign tourist to be able to flag down a passing cab or tuk-tuk or a *songthaew* (a shared-ride truck common in Thailand). After a while, he gave up.

- He also tried telephoning for taxis, but the only firm which would respond was the one whose taxis were lined up outside the hotel. They still wanted a lot more money for a short ride than any other taxi service which my friend had used in his extensive travels around Thailand.

- He thought of renting a car, but to do so would have been much more expensive than paying the taxi drivers what they wanted, and in any case, the idea of driving on the left in a country where rules of the road are seldom followed was not appealing.

- He tried walking, but that was no fun in the hot and humid Thai weather along the side of a busy road.

In the end, he was forced to pay the taxi mafia what it wanted. Though he probably did not lose more than $60 to the taxi mafia during his stay, he vowed never to go to Phuket again.

Phuket's taxi mafia problem has been acknowledged by the local government for quite some time. In 2005, the Governor said that in one part of the island, tuk-tuks were not letting anybody else on their turf. He thought that metering might solve some of the problems, but acknowledged that it was unlikely to be a complete solution, since taxi drivers could simply refuse to use their meters.

Despite the Governor's intervention, reports from swindled tourists continued. In 2014, the Thai Government decided to send in the Army in a show of force. A deployment of 100 soldiers from Southern Thailand provided military support to a huge task force of 1,110 police officers and 40 volunteers who swept along the west coast of Phuket to purge the island of illegal, violent, abusive and cheating taxi, tuk-tuk and minivan drivers. Internet forums are divided on whether the military crackdown has made any difference or not.

Taxi mafia stories from elsewhere

There are plenty of stories of organised overcharged by taxis in tourist cities around the world. Simply Googling the name of a tourist city, with "taxi mafia", will often generate plenty of stories. Here are some more instances, though after a while, they are all variations on a theme:

- In Prague, sources reported organised overcharging by taxi drivers around the tourist hotspots of the Charles Bridge and St Wenceslas Square.

- In Nice, the taxi mafia seems well-entrenched, and has done its best to set fares to the airport as high as possible and ban competition from Uber.

- In Bali, Indonesia, the taxi mafia is estimated to steal hundreds of thousands of dollars a year from tourists visiting the island.

- In Goa, India, taxi drivers are described as exploitative, and aggressive towards their customers, and their fares exorbitant.

14. Other taxi scams

Likely damage: 3/5

Frequency: 2/5

Countries reported: Global.

Summary: Miscellaneous scams by taxi drivers on tourists: driving off with their luggage, short-changing them, and so on.

One scam which taxi drivers sometimes try to pull off is simple:

1. A tourist arrives at the train station or airport of a foreign city. She hails a taxi cab, putting her bag into the trunk of the vehicle, which drives off to the tourist's destination.

2. Either the meter, if any, seems to be working, or else the tourist has negotiated a reasonable fare for the journey.

3. The ride ends and the tourist gets out and pays the taxi driver. She walks out of the taxi to retrieve his bag.

4. The taxi driver simply drives off, taking the luggage.

This can be devastating. Unless she carried a daypack or money belt with her, with all her money and credit cards, the victim has just lost everything.

A taxi driver robbed a friend of mine in another way:

1. She had hired a taxi on arrival at the airport in Lima, Peru, to take her to her hotel.

2. She put her main suitcase in the trunk of the taxi and shut it, then put her smaller backpack, which contained all her valuables, on top. She got into the taxi.

3. The driver claimed that the trunk was not closed. He got out, walked around the taxi and opened and closed the trunk, apparently with some difficulty.

4. While he was doing this, he must have opened her backpack, put his hand in it, and stolen her camera and some cash. She was sitting in the taxi so she saw nothing.

My friend only realised what had happened much later when she looked inside her backpack inside her hotel room, by which time, of course, the taxi driver was long gone.

A scam reported from some Latin American and Asian countries is also relatively simple and much less damaging:

1. The victim hires a taxi and tells the driver the destination.

2. On the way, the driver notices that he is running low on fuel. He therefore stops to buy some.

3. When the time comes to pay, however, he finds out that he does not have the correct change.

4. He asks the victim to "lend" him, say, $5 to pay the attendant? He promises to deduct it from the fare. The implicit threat, of course, is that if the victim does not pay, he will be delayed, as the driver will have an argument with the cashier. The driver is calculating that the victim may well forget to deduct $5 from the fare at the end of the taxi ride, especially if it is long, or if the victim is clearly tired or drunk.

Another relatively trivial scam seems to be worldwide:

1. A tourist hires a taxi, arrives at his destination and prepares to pay. Unfortunately, he only has a banknote much larger than the fare. He expects to be given change.

2. The taxi driver says, however, that he has no change. He is clearly hoping that the tourist will tell him not to worry about the

change, thereby giving him a large tip. If the tourist is in a hurry, he may well be tempted to pay up. If the driver really is running low on change, however, he should have told his passenger before he started on the journey.

When a tourist is going to an isolated destination in a country, where taxis are not metered, the taxi driver may ask his passenger to pay again once they have arrived at the tourist's destination. He will use the excuse that he has to return, and there are no customers for him at the isolated destination. There is no reason why a passenger should pay for the taxi driver to return, especially as he has only made this clear once he has dropped his victim off – if the driver was going to ask him to pay twice for the same journey, he should have done so when the tourist got into his cab, rather than when he dropped his victim off.

So, here are some general rules when dealing with taxis:

1. Keep hand luggage with you inside the cab, not in the trunk.

2. Retrieve your luggage before you pay the taxi driver.

3. Try to make sure you have a mix of currency, to avoid breaking a large bank note.

15. Thieving baggage handlers

Likely damage: 3/5

Frequency: 2/5

Countries reported: Global.

Summary: How baggage handlers steal from tourists' bags at airports.

Travellers entrust their baggage to airport authorities every time they fly, unless they are travelling with hand baggage only. This, in effect, means that they entrust it to the airline, the airport and their baggage handlers. At some airports, the baggage handlers are employees of the airport, whilst at others they are employees of the airline. Virtually every airport in the world has tales of theft by baggage handlers, and those that do not have probably not been proactive enough to catch them.

Since 2003, the Transportation Security Agency (TSA), which screens checked baggage in the United States, has received more than 70,000 complaints about theft from suitcases. A CNN analysis of passenger property loss claims, filed with the TSA from 2010 to 2014, estimated 30,621 claims of missing valuables. At Bangkok's Suvarnabhumi Airport, the problem is so bad that baggage handlers were issued with uniforms with no pockets, so they could not hide stolen items in their clothing. Most baggage handlers are honest, but a sufficient number are dishonest that many regular travellers have stories of losing their property from their checked suitcases.

Stealing from passengers' suitcases has been made much easier by the regulations designed to allow security screening. In order to enable cases to be checked for contraband and explosives, some travellers are now usually forbidden to lock them. Some travellers still lock them, but those that do risk having their locks broken or their cases destroyed. Travellers in the United States can use special locks which TSA employees can open using master keys, but unfortunately some TSA employees are themselves dishonest. In addition to stealing cases, baggage handlers can also damage them.

There are a number of tips to minimize the risk of theft from checked suitcases:

1. The best way to avoid losing items of value from checked suitcases is not to put them in there in the first place. It is very unwise to put electronic goods such as laptops or expensive cameras in checked baggage. Cash and vital documents should

never be checked, nor should expensive clothes unless there is no alternative. It should all be carried in hand luggage.

2. If there is no alternative, either because yet another terrorist scare has caused airports to restrict further what may be taken onboard the airplane with you, or because you are carrying too many items as hand luggage, it is best to bury expensive items as deeply as possible.

3. Surround valuables with underwear or socks if possible, to make it as difficult as possible for crooked baggage handlers to find them.

4. Expensive-looking cases are most likely to attract attention, so do not buy the most expensive type.

5. If your baggage is lost, broken into or stolen, it is important to report it to the airline at the airport at the time, rather than leaving the airport and coming back.

6. Ensure that you keep the baggage claim tag, as it is your only proof that you checked in any bags in the first place.

7. If you are sure items have been stolen, file a police report with the police at the airport, who most likely deal with similar problems all the time. Under the Warsaw Convention, if the whole bag is stolen/goes missing, airlines are required to compensate their passengers if their bags are not found. Many give the passenger a daily allowance until the bags are found again.

Baggage handlers charged in Las Vegas

In February 2017, three baggage handlers were charged with multiple felonies for stealing from customers' luggage at McCarran International Airport in Las Vegas. The thefts occurred over several months and included items such as luxury purses and guns. Detectives tied the thefts to the accused using data from their key cards that helped track their movements. Investigators then obtained a list of items reported stolen and matched them up with similar items sold by the accused to local pawn shops. One of the defendants told police that stealing from luggage was a common practice among his colleagues and admitted to taking and pawning several items, arrest reports said.

Baggage handlers investigated in Hawaii

In 2016, three men were arrested and dozens of others investigated by the FBI and the Bureau of Alcohol, Tobacco and Firearms. The men were baggage handlers at Kahului airport in Maui. The investigation was triggered when two law enforcement officers noticed that their guns had been stolen. As proof that no articles are immune from theft, another man lost hundreds of dollars in dried fish and fish hooks.

30 Portuguese baggage handlers charged with theft

In July 2016, 30 Portuguese baggage handlers were charged with theft for stealing numerous low-value items including electronics, jewellery and even clothes. The criminals seemed fairly sophisticated. They collaborated in small groups. One stayed on watch, while the others opened the luggage. The crimes were committed in the hold of the aircraft. When the teams left planes whose luggage they had robbed, they hid stolen booty in their lockers. They used the dead angles in the airport's CCTV system to their advantage. One member of the team had two machines for smelting that were used to transform stolen gold. Passengers using Lisbon airport were advised to secure their cases with padlocks.

16. Airport scanner scam

Likely damage: 3/5

Frequency: 2/5

Countries reported: Global.

Summary: How teams of scammers steal your hand luggage while it is going through the X-ray machine.

Airports are some of the most heavily controlled and policed buildings on the planet. As security continues to tighten in most countries, it is becoming more difficult for criminals who are not employed by the airport to steal from tourists there. This scam, which involves stealing from travellers as they go through airport scanners, seems to be relatively rare, and indeed some people doubt that it occurs at all. If it is an urban myth, however, it is a persistent one: I was warned about it when I was issued with my laptop while training for my first job in 1996.

Millions of people pass through the scanners at airport security each week around the world. They are also required to put whatever items of hand luggage they are flying with through X-ray machines. This has opened the way for teams of two scammers to try to steal passengers' hand luggage while they are separated from it, as follows:

1. The scammers will target a traveller who seems to have valuable hand luggage.

2. Two criminals will stand in front of their target in the line for security search. The criminal who stands in the line first will be the thief. The second of the criminals will leave lots of metal items in his pockets to ensure that he is stopped by airport security.

3. The first criminal will go through security and wait at the other end. The passenger (our mark) will put his briefcase or laptop bag on the conveyor belt to be X-rayed. The case will go through the scanner.

4. The second criminal will be stopped and frisked so the mark will be delayed.

5. While he is waiting for the second criminal to be frisked and sent on his way, the first criminal will walk off with the mark's case, which has already come through.

6. Because the victim is waiting for the second criminal to clear security, he will probably not be watching his case. In the unlikely event that he notices the first criminal has walked off with his case and attempts to alert security, the first criminal can always claim that he picked the case up by mistake, as so many cases look alike.

The Kenyan police warn against this scam on their website, particularly as thieves are likely to steal laptop computers. They recommend carrying the laptop in a non-descript case, only putting the laptop on the conveyor belt for the scanner when you are next in line, about to be searched, and keeping your eye on your laptop as it comes off the conveyor belt. The US Federal Aviation Administration has also issued warnings against this scam.

Airports are also good places for thieves to distract passengers and steal their goods, or else to steal the bags of passengers who are already distracted. See the example below for how a couple lost $590,000 (!) of jewellery in this way in 1997. Some thieves apparently buy plane tickets with many airport stopovers and commit multiple thefts at each airport. Unless a thief is caught red-handed, by the time the thefts have been reported to airport security and the police (and the thief has been identified) he will likely be gone.

Worst airports for laptop theft

A 2011 report by Absolute.com listed the 20 worst airports globally for laptop theft (not just in airport security, but throughout the airport). The top 13 airports were all in the United States, with Atlanta winning the title of the worst facility. Miami,

Chicago and Houston were runners up. Frankfurt was the worst non-US airport surveyed.

$590,000 theft at Newark airport security

Elyse Lanier, the wife of Houston's popular mayor and real estate developer Bob Lanier, had been shopping in New York, where she had bought $590,000 of jewellery. The couple were heading home through Newark Airport. Mrs Lanier was distracted by a man, whose accomplices then bumped into her. They pointed to an airline ticket folder on the floor. Mrs Lanier stooped to pick it up and examined it. Her bag was taken from the conveyor belt while she was stooping down. When she looked up, the thieves were gone. Of course, an episode like this could easily have been an inside job.

17. Armed robberies near airports

Likely damage: 4/5

Frequency: 1/5

Countries reported: Mexico, Venezuela, South Africa.

Summary: Travellers are followed and held up after changing money at airports.

Closely related to scam #22 (muggings at ATMs) is the practice of watching tourists who change money at a bureau de change, following them, and then mugging them. It seems to be most common at bureaux de change at Caracas airport in Venezuela and in Mexico City (see example below). Although it has been reported in particular from these two Latin American countries, there does not seem to be anything preventing it from spreading.

A number of criminals are involved in this scam. It works as follows:

1. One scammer observes the tourists at the counter changing money. He chooses a tourist who seems to be changing a lot of cash.

2. Once the victim has got his cash, the first criminal follows him, noting the number of the car or taxi which he uses. He then calls his accomplices on a cell phone, tipping them off about which cab the victim is in.

3. The accomplices of the first man then follow the victim's car or taxi.

4. The airport will probably be too heavily policed for a safe robbery. The scammers therefore wait until the victim has left it. They stop the victim's car somehow, and demand the cash.

5. If the victim refuses to hand over his cash, the scammers threaten him. If he continues to refuse, things may turn nasty as we shall see in the example from Mexico City below.

Avoiding this scam is difficult if you use bureaux de change after you leave customs at the airport. Most of us are not trained to know when we are being watched. We will not notice thieves tipping off their accomplices by making calls on their cell phones. There are steps that you can take, however, if you are in an area notorious for this scam:

- When using ATMs, the advice is always to "be aware of your surroundings", noting anybody or anything which seems to be out of place. This is also good advice when using bureaux de change if the city which you are in has a bad reputation for theft or mugging.

- Do not withdraw or change a large amount of cash at once. Thieves are less likely to target travellers who withdraw a small amount of money.

- If you change money before you fly, you will not need to use ATMs or bureaux de change in airports. Bear in mind that certain countries (including India) have controlled currencies meaning you cannot obtain their currency overseas. In other words, you have to change your money when you arrive.

- It is certainly better to hand over money immediately when threatened with a weapon. Any life is worth far more than a few hundred, or even a few thousand, dollars. Now and again, people take on armed muggers and manage to capture them or alert the police, but these people are obviously taking a huge risk. Having been mugged myself by a man with a machete, however, I can say that in situations like that it is extremely difficult to think rationally. The adrenalin flooded my system and I felt extremely angry. I am glad, however, that I handed over the money and escaped uninjured.

Robbery of a tourist in Johannesburg

In February 2017, thieves robbed a tourist in Johannesburg, South Africa. The men had followed the tourist from OR Tambo airport and robbed him at gunpoint outside his guesthouse in the suburb of Edleen. They got away with $2,000. When the manager of the guesthouse ran out to help the tourist, the thieves told him to go back inside or they would shoot him.

Robbery of a diplomat in Johannesburg

A Kenyan diplomat was followed from the same OR Tambo airport and robbed outside of an upmarket estate in Centurion in September 2016. The diplomat, his wife, a driver and the official were waiting to get into the estate when their car was ambushed by two armed men. A third man was driving the robbers' getaway car. Three guards at the gate were overwhelmed, made to lie on the ground, and robbed. The officials' suitcases, laptops, phones and documents were stolen.

Thieves target tourists who change money at Mexico City airport

In January 2009, a 55-year-old French tourist was shot in the head in Mexico City. He had changed money on arrival at the airport then hailed a taxi. According to the Frenchman's driver, two cars appeared to follow them after they left the airport, then cut them off. One man got out of one of the cars and demanded the tourist's money at gunpoint. When the tourist refused, he was shot and more than $6,000/£5,000 was stolen. He was taken to hospital where he was later reported to be alive but in a "serious" condition.

According to Mexican police, three similar robberies had taken place in Mexico City in the months before this shooting.

Fake police officers at Johannesburg Airport

In 2009, four Turkish nationals were arrested at OR Tambo Airport in Johannesburg, South Africa for impersonating police officers and targeting wealthy-looking tourists as they arrived. The fake police would follow their victims, pull their cars over and tell their victims that they were drugs or tourist police. They would then search the tourists' luggage and steal their laptops and jewellery. Four men were arrested in 2007 for similar crimes at the same airport.

18. Ticket inspector scams

Likely damage: 2/5

Frequency: 2/5

Countries reported: Poland, Czech Republic, Hungary, Bulgaria.

Summary: Overzealous and fraudulent ticket inspectors rip tourists off on subways and buses all over Eastern Europe.

This scam is reported from Eastern Europe in particular, and hundreds, or perhaps thousands, of travellers must be caught by it each year. It works as follows:

1. Overly zealous and excessively efficient ticket inspectors target travellers on Eastern European subways and buses, relying on their victims not knowing the rules concerning buying and validating tickets, which are often slightly different from back home.

2. The tourist is, of course, likely to have bought a ticket, but may not have bought the correct ticket, and even if they have bought the correct ticket, may not have validated it (i.e. stamped it using one of the machines in the Metro stations, to cancel it before they get on). Tickets do not generally have to be validated in British, French or American subway or bus systems.

3. The inspectors then levy fines, part of which they keep.

4. Most countries will cut foreigners extra slack, understanding that it is unreasonable to expect them to know the rules as well as locals, but in Eastern Europe, foreigners are targeted because they generally have more money than the locals.

While locals are subject to scamming in this way, tourists are much less likely to know the rules of the system. The more complicated these are, the easier it is for tourists to be caught out. I have been caught out in this way twice in Eastern Europe (see below).

I have heard from other travellers in Eastern Europe who have had similar fines levied on them. It does seem to be an Eastern European speciality. In Western Europe, the only time I have unintentionally violated ticketing laws (in Munich) and been caught, the inspector realised that I was not familiar with the local rules, and contented himself with explaining them to me. The officials in Eastern Europe want your money – they do not necessarily want to inconvenience you or lock you up. If you really do not want to pay the fine, it is possible that, if you can refuse long enough, they will let you go because while they are talking to you, they are missing the opportunity to demand more fines from other passengers.

I have also heard from travellers in Prague and Budapest of another scam related to subway ticket inspectors:

1. Occasionally, fraudulent ticket inspectors turn up at subway stations and target tourists, who are less likely to know the rules, rather than locals.

2. They will stop a tourist, take his valid ticket, and invent a reason why the ticket is not valid.

3. They will levy the fine and hope that the tourist pays instead of asking to be taken to the police station.

As long as officials can demand fines in cash from people for breaking rules of which they were not aware, or which they do not understand, and receive a commission from the money they take in (or even keep all of it), they will be tempted to target groups less likely to understand. Knowing the rules makes it more difficult for them to target you. As my Sofia experience showed me (see below), even if you think you have followed them entirely, officials can still sometimes use or invent rules of which you were not aware. Fortunately, this scam is not particularly damaging, though it is widespread and annoying in Eastern European cities.

Fake ticket inspector swindles dozens in Prague

A man pretended to be a ticket inspector in Prague. He would offer to extend the validity of tourists' fare cards (called the OpenCard in Prague) if they gave him 500 Czech crowns ($20/£16). He used a fake reader connected to a mobile phone, which would print off a "confirmation" that the OpenCard had been extended for a year. He would approach people on trams, in nightclubs and in shopping malls. Police estimated that he could have had hundreds of victims.

Fraudulent ticket inspectors in Paris

In March 2014, an English couple were at the Eurostar terminal in Paris. Two men, claiming to be ticket inspectors, demanded their tickets and declared that they were invalid. This would mean a €33 "on the spot fine". The Englishman refused to pay, there ensued a heated confrontation, and eventually he demanded that the inspectors called the police. At which point, apparently, they decided that they had had enough, so they left them alone.

Zealous ticket inspector in Budapest, Hungary

In Budapest, 20 years ago, I was travelling with two people. We had bought tickets to travel on the Metro (which then cost about ten or fifteen cents). We had not, however, realised that we had to validate the tickets using one of the machines in the Metro before we got on. We boarded the Metro, travelled four stops, and got off at the main station, Deak Ferenc Ter, where all three of Budapest's metro lines came together. We got off the train and went up the escalator. It is built in such a way that you cannot see the top from the bottom, and it seems to be a favourite spot for ticket inspectors.

Just after we reached the top of the escalators, we were accosted by two elderly ladies who demanded our tickets, in broken English. It was fairly clear, from the way we had been stopped, that they had been targeting tourists – with our cameras around our necks, our English-language T-shirts and our shorts and flip-flops! We showed one of the women our tickets. As she saw they had not been validated, her eyes lit up. She became extremely aggressive and demanded money from each of us. We did not understand what we had done wrong, and argued with her for a while. She was very persistent in demanding the fines from us, which, I think, were about $4 each.

Eventually, another passenger, who was Hungarian but spoke English, stopped and told us that he had seen foreigners being caught many times in this way, and that it would be much quicker to pay up. He explained that we had to get our tickets validated before travel, since the tickets were not date or time-stamped when we bought them, and otherwise we could, in theory, use the same ticket for travelling on the Metro indefinitely. We grimaced, paid up, and grumbled about it to each other for the next hour.

Swindling ticket inspectors in Sofia, Bulgaria

The second time I was caught by Eastern European ticket inspectors was in Bulgaria in 2006. I was at the end of a good trip, travelling overland from Budapest through Romania down to Sofia, Bulgaria's capital. I was on my way to the airport for my flight home on the local city bus. I had bought a ticket and validated it in the machine. The bus was almost empty besides myself. I had put my case on the seat next to me. About halfway through the journey to the airport, two public transport revenue controllers boarded the bus, and demanded my ticket. I handed it over. However, they aggressively demanded a second ticket. It took me some time to work out why.

It turned out that they were arguing that, as my bag was on the seat, I was required to have a second ticket for it, even though the bus, besides myself and my suitcase, was completely empty. I was very surprised. I had never heard of this rule in any public bus company anywhere in the world, and it did not even occur to me that it might be a problem. They demanded an on-the-spot fine of, if memory serves, about $5. I had actually spent almost all my Bulgarian money, and they said that I would have to go to the police station if I could not pay. This would have entailed, at least, missing my flight. Fortunately, I just about managed to rustle up the money they demanded in change. I paid the fine and they went away. I have no idea if the rule they cited existed or whether they were just making it up to demand an "on-the-spot fine" from me.

19. False fellow traveller scams

Likely damage: 4/5

Frequency: 2/5

Countries reported: Global.

Summary: Scammers pretend to be tourists, meet other tourists, befriend them and then rob them.

One scam, which takes place largely at the more budget end of the travel industry, targets the large number of people who travel by themselves, though it is certainly possible for couples or larger groups to be ripped off in this way. Many places around the world have well-established budget tourist routes, such as the Garden Route along the southern coast of South Africa, or the Gringo Trail along the Andes in South America. For many single travellers, meeting and travelling with fellow independent travellers can be one of the most enjoyable parts of the whole trip. In a holiday lasting several months, a single traveller can meet, and travel with, dozens of other tourists. It is not surprising, therefore, that a few of their new "friends" may actively seek to scam them. Travelling with somebody else, even for a couple of days, can be an intimate experience. I have heard it described as being more intense than a marriage, since married couples are usually apart while one or both of them is at work. Travelling companions are often with each other every waking hour, and indeed every sleeping hour too, if they keep costs down by sharing a hotel room. The very closeness of this relationship gives many opportunities for scamming a fellow traveller.

From conversations with tourist police and hotel managers, I have heard about a type of person who makes his living from meeting travellers on public transport or in cheap accommodation:

1. Once they have gained the trust of their new companions, they rip them off in some way. They may steal the victims' valuables when they are not looking, or steal their identities, making copies of their credit cards and passports and selling them to gangs of criminals.

2. Once the theft has taken place, the false friend may then vanish.

3. He may attempt to blame unknown thieves or another traveller for the theft, but will then disappear and pick on another victim in a different part of the country.

The number of scammers in any group of travellers is very small. The vast majority of fellow travellers are sincere and genuine, and often extremely interesting, friendly and helpful. Nevertheless, many people have been robbed by travelling companions whom they trusted, and a few have had even worse experiences (see the examples below). Their companion may, for instance, have attempted to plant drugs on them, so that the victim carries them through an international border (as a so-called drugs mule), and takes the blame if they are found.

False travellers tend to target people who travel cheaply because they (the false travellers) often do not have the money to stay in the expensive places where people who travel more expensively are to be found. In addition, cheap hotels and hostels tend to be rather more easy-going about security. As by far the largest group of false travellers seems to consist of young men, it is easiest for them to ingratiate themselves with other young people, who tend to travel cheaply. This is not to say that travellers on high budgets should automatically trust everybody: they should perhaps be aware that they can make more tempting targets, since they usually have more to steal.

There is no way to avoid the possibility of being robbed by other travellers completely, but it is certainly possible to cut down the risk. The obvious way to make it less likely that the stranger you have just met, and are contemplating travelling with, will not scam you is to get to know them before you travel. "Reading" people, trying to judge their thoughts and motivations, is a skill at which nobody can ever be perfect at, though some people seem naturally gifted at it. It is a very useful skill in many situations, but particularly when deciding whether to trust somebody. Meeting lots of people from different countries around the world is a very good way of improving people-reading abilities, and a powerful incentive is the need to judge when somebody is likely to scam you.

It is certainly a good idea to ask anybody you plan to travel with a number of questions, in a friendly, non-confrontational way, before you commit to anything, or leave your valuables with them. Obvious questions include:

- What they do for a living back home?

- Where are they coming from?

- Where are they going to?

- What have they done in previous locations?

- Do they always travel alone or have they travelled with others previously?

Most travellers like nothing better than talking about their travels (the great difficulty is often in shutting them up!), so you do not need to feel that you are being intrusive or rude. Vague or inconsistent answers should raise immediate red, or at least yellow, flags. Evasive or shifty looks, or similar, worrying, body language, are also obvious danger signs. Somebody who seems too willing to forget his travel plans and follow yours may, of course, simply like you a lot, but may also have selected you as his next victim and want to scam you.

Nobody can ever know for certain what is going on in someone else's head, and therefore it is important not to rely totally on your people-reading skills to determine whether to travel with somebody you have just met or not. Here are some tips, based on my experience of travelling with people (none of whom, in decades of travelling, have ever ripped me off):

- Do not leave your most valuable possessions (cash, electronic goods, passport and so on) with your new travelling companion.

- NEVER agree to carry their bags or other possessions across borders, as they could contain drugs or other illegal goods.

- It is important to realise that, when you meet someone, just because they do not intend to rip you off when you start travelling together, does not mean that they will always respect your property. They may decide later on to steal a number of your possessions. This kind of temptation can be too much for a weak nature. They may not even do it for the financial reward as much as the thrill it gives them.

- Lock your valuables away when you go to sleep if possible, and keep them on you, or in your sight, as much as you can during the day.

Australian traveller robbed in India

In 2015, an Australian traveller met an Indian man at Mumbai airport. He chatted her up and claimed to have no money. She offered to lend him $200. They would meet again some weeks later and he would repay her. However, he never showed up, and she never saw her money again.

Australian says he was tricked into smuggling drugs into China

On March 11, 2014, Australian Anthony Bannister was found with 3 kg of crystal meth in eight ladies' handbags in his luggage in Guangzhou. In 2015, he was given a suspended death sentence for smuggling the drugs into China. Bannister said he was tricked by a sophisticated drugs syndicate who groomed him online, lured him to Guangzhou on false pretences, and handed him a piece of luggage to bring back with him at the last minute. Twelve other Australians were incarcerated in China for similar crimes which could attract the death penalty. Many of them were also claiming that the drugs had been planted on them in various ways.

False friends rob and murder tourists in Bolivia

According to the US embassy in La Paz:

"[A fake] 'tourist' will befriend the victims and might seek assistance in some manner. After a period of time, [fake] 'police' intercept the victims and the 'tourist'.

At this point, the 'police' discover some sort of contraband (usually drugs) on the 'tourist'. The entire group is then taken to the 'police station'. At this point, the 'police' seize the documents, credit cards, and ATM cards of the victims. The perpetrators obtain PIN numbers, sometimes by threat of violence, and the scam is complete.

Another technique again introduces a 'tourist' to the victims. This 'tourist' can be any race or gender and will probably be able to speak the language of the victims. This meeting can happen anywhere and the goal of the 'tourist' is to build the trust of the victims. Once a certain level of trust is obtained, the 'tourist' suggests a particular mode of transportation to a location (usually a taxi). The 'taxi' picks up the victims and the 'tourist' and delivers the group to a safe house in the area. At this point the victims are informed that they are now kidnapped and are forced to give up their credit cards and ATM cards with pin numbers [i.e. PINs]".

British false fellow traveller kills three

In 1995, British fellow traveller John Martin Scripps befriended and murdered at least three tourists: two Canadians in Thailand, and one South African in Singapore. He would accost them at airports and try to befriend them. Once they had let their guard down sufficiently, he killed them in their hotel rooms. He stole their valuables and credit cards and cut up their bodies in an attempt to disguise his crimes. He was convicted of the murder of the South African in Singapore and executed in 1996.

---

20. Theft from buses' luggage holds

Likely damage: 3/5

Frequency: 1/5

Countries reported: Global, particularly Latin America and South East Asia.

Summary: Thieves steal checked baggage during bus journeys.

In many countries, long distance buses are the most common, and often the only, form of inter-city transport. Where there are no trains, and where flights are either not available, or too expensive, travellers often have a choice between renting a car and going by bus. Even if they can afford to rent a car, if they are going one way they may not want to go back to return it, and so they are often forced to go by bus. Bus travel is often cheap and sometimes even comfortable, especially in some South American countries. It can also be fast, providing the roads are decent, though it can be extremely slow and uncomfortable if they are not.

In many countries, long-distance buses are notorious for theft. One common scam works as follows:

1. As with airlines, passengers must check large bags, which are then stowed in the hold.

2. The bus is likely to make intermediate stops.

3. It is relatively easy for the thief simply to claim the traveller's bag as his own if he gets off before his victim does. He can then help himself to whatever is in the bag.

It is such an easy scam to pull off that I am surprised it does not happen more often, especially on those bus routes with lots of tourists. In some countries, it clearly has been attempted many times, and many bus companies give their customers a receipt or ticket for their suitcases when those bags are stowed in the hold of the bus. Not all bus companies do this, however, and if they do not, travellers' suitcases can be stolen whenever the bus stops.

Another form of theft occurs with the cooperation of the bus driver. It works as follows:

1. On the larger buses, the baggage holds are easily large enough to hold a person as well as a suitcase or two for everybody on board. Many such buses have a porter who takes tourists' bags and puts them in the hold.

2. When the bus is about to leave, the porter simply gets into the hold and closes the door. He will have a flashlight and probably some pliers.

3. The porter goes through all the bags, stealing anything of value, and get off when the bus stops for the first time, before the passengers have had time to leave the bus.

The passengers will probably not know of the thefts until they reach their hotel rooms, by which time the thief will be long gone.

I have heard of a similar, related, scam, being practised in Central America and South East Asia. It relies on the fact that many long-distance buses have doors to their baggage holds on both sides.

1. The thieves, with the cooperation of the bus driver, stop the bus, saying that it has broken down.

2. They point the passengers in the direction of a place to sit on one side of the bus while it is repaired.

3. While all the travellers are on one side of the bus, the thieves open the baggage hold doors on the other side and steal all the passengers' possessions.

Theft on a night bus in Thailand

A friend was on a night bus in Thailand. He was sleeping peacefully. The bus apparently broke down in the middle of the night and all the passengers were ordered off and pushed to one side of the road. While they were standing there, the other side of the bus was apparently opened and some of their bags were stolen, more or less in front of their noses. The theft was not discovered until they reached their destination.

Chapter 3: Cash, ATM and credit card scams

When travelling, tourists often carry more cash with them than they would at home. They may want to eat in nice restaurants, buy expensive souvenirs, or otherwise indulge themselves. They also carry more cash than the locals. This makes them rich pickings for thieves, who know very well that mugging a tourist may be much more profitable than mugging a local. As an added bonus for the criminals, tourists are less likely to complain about losing cash than about having their camera stolen, as cash is often not covered by travel insurance policies. Thieves love handling cash, because it is very easy to get rid of, and difficult to trace.

Card fraud (a term covering both ATM debit and credit cards) is a rapidly growing crime in many countries. More people are paying for their purchases with credit cards, and, if they can get hold of the all-important card numbers and PINs, thieves can loot people's accounts without being found out for weeks or months, giving them the chance to conceal their identities. Thieves often target people when they are at their most vulnerable. In one particularly pernicious example of this breed of scam, sleeping guests at a hotel receive a phone call from people claiming to work at the hotel reception. The victims are informed that their card details have been lost: can they please give their card number, expiry date, and so on. If the guest does so, thousands are spent on his account before he gets out of bed.

21. "Too many zeros" scams

Likely damage: 3/5

Frequency: 1/5

Countries reported: Romania, Turkey, Italy, Indonesia.

Summary: Scammers take advantage of currencies with lots of zeros or old banknotes to confuse tourists.

Many countries have had, until recently, currencies which meant that you need thousands or millions of that currency to pay for a short taxi ride, or a bar of candy. Many more still do. They provide tourists from other countries with the mild thrill of being multi-millionaires or even billionaires for a few days. But they also provide many opportunities to scam people who are less familiar with the difficult calculations involved in using these currencies than the thieves are.

Most people can still be a millionaire in Japan, where a million yen is worth around $12,000/£8,000 but most other tourists come from countries with stable currencies, like the Eurozone or America, and in everyday life only use up to 50 dollar or euro notes. Americans and Europeans can therefore be easily baffled by the maths involved in spending millions of Indonesian rupiah to buy an expensive watch or a plane ticket.

One of the best opportunities for scamming occurs when the old currency with all the zeros is replaced by a new currency. For a while, old notes and new notes exist together. Scammers can pass off an almost worthless note in the old currency as a valuable note in the new currency. An example of how this worked in Romania in 2005 is given in the first example below.

Another, far simpler, way of taking advantage of a currency with lots of zeros does not need the revaluation of the currency, or any complicated switching between new notes and old. It is simply to use the number of zeroes used for everyday transactions to give the wrong change by a factor of ten. When ten million is required, the hustler gives a million back. Money changers often use this scam (see scam #24). Most people's brains are not used to performing calculations involving many zeroes. If the victim spots the scam, the missing nine million can be given and nothing is lost, while if the victim does not spot the scam, the hustler has made a lot of money. It is a good scam from the criminal's point of view because it is easy to make an honest mistake when dealing with lots of zeroes, so it's very difficult to prove the swindle, even if there are lots of witnesses.

At the time of writing, there are no currency revaluations planned around the world. The position changes all the time, however, and the way to avoid these scams is to be aware of the currency situation in the country you are visiting – a quick Internet search should reveal any changes planned. Besides those in the examples below, recent currency revaluations have included:

- Ghana in 2007, where the new Ghanaian cedi is worth 10,000 old Ghanaian cedis.

- North Korea in 2009, which revalued its currency by a factor of 100.

Here is a list of the countries where almost everybody can still be a millionaire. Tourists need to watch the zeroes, or carry a calculator, in:

- West Africa (613 CFA francs to the US dollar)

- Chile (656 Chilean pesos to the US dollar)

- Colombia (2,922 Colombian pesos to the US dollar)

- Costa Rica (547 Costa Rican colones to the US dollar)

- Hungary (289 Hungarian forints to the US dollar)

- Indonesia (13,400 Indonesian rupiah to the US dollar)

- Jamaica (129 Jamaican dollars to the US dollar)

- Kenya (104 Kenyan shillings to the US dollar)

- Lebanon (1,513 Lebanese pounds to the US dollar)

- Laos (8,206 Lao kips to the US dollar)

- Pakistan (105 Pakistani rupees to the US dollar)

- Paraguay (5,781 Paraguayan Guarani to the US dollar)

- Sri Lanka (150 Sri Lankan rupees to the US dollar)

- Vietnam (22,650 Vietnamese dong to the US dollar)

Note: the above exchange rates were correct at the time of writing. Source: xe.com

Scams following a recent currency revaluation in Romania

In Romania in 2005, the government decided to knock three zeroes off the old currency, so that a thousand old lei became one new leu. Locals, who have lived with the old notes all their lives, know which are which, and quickly get used to dealing with both forms of money. Tourists may not. Their guidebooks are often published years before the change in currency, and in any case, few of them bother to read the relevant sections. I was in Romania while the old and the new currencies were circulating together. I met several travellers there who had been tricked, usually by taxi drivers, into handing over hundreds of new banknotes, and being given change in almost worthless old lei. The average loss seemed to be about €300/$400 – enough to dent most people's budgets. Given the sums involved, it would have been easy to lose far more. I must say, most of them took it rather better than I would have!

Fewer scams following a Turkish revaluation

Also in 2005, the Turkish government decided to revalue its currency, knocking six zeroes off, so that one million old lira was worth one new lira. In this case, however, the difference between the old and the new currencies was so enormous that scamming was more difficult, and I heard of no travellers caught out this way when I passed through Istanbul shortly after the revaluation. Even the most mathematically incompetent person would think it odd to be asked for a thousand or ten thousand dollars' worth of

Turkish currency and to be given notes of a hundred thousand or a million lira in change.

22. ATM muggings

Likely damage: 4/5

Frequency: 2/5

Countries reported: Global.

Summary: Travellers are mugged after using ATMs for their cards and PINs.

In all but the most remote countries, it is possible to take money from your bank account using an ATM. These machines have spread worldwide in the past three decades, and it is certainly convenient to be able to withdraw hundreds of dollars or pounds per day from a home bank account, almost anywhere in the world. In places where ATMs are not yet widespread, particularly in poor countries off the tourist trail, it is often necessary to carry enough US dollars or euros in cash to last for the entire trip, or else to use travellers' cheques, which are often difficult, and sometimes impossible, to cash.

The overwhelming majority of visits to ATMs are trouble free. However, local criminals in many countries have noticed that travellers use ATMs, and have made it their business to rob them. If a criminal can get hold of an ATM or credit card number and the associated PIN, he can empty the account as quickly as the bank will let him. The victim is very unlikely to know that she has been scammed in this way until either:

- She checks her bank balance and notices lots of unexplained withdrawals; or

- Her bank freezes her card, leaving her without access to her money until she calls them. Of course, banks never seem to consider how she is supposed to call them from overseas without money from her account.

People experience this scam at home as well, but there the problem can be easier to sort out than when overseas. Without another source of money, losing an ATM card while abroad can be a major disaster – I have been caught out in this way myself, and have had to rely on others' help to survive. It is easier for the bank to send a new card to an existing address than for them to send it to you while you are travelling. It may also be more difficult for you to check your bank balance regularly if you are away from the Internet and phones while travelling. Above all, most people, while travelling, are not thinking of checking their bank balances, and are therefore less likely to note that their account is being looted.

There are a number of ways for thieves to scam travellers while they are using ATMs. However, in the most common crime of this type:

1. The criminals approach someone using an ATM when there is nobody around, usually but not necessarily at night.

2. The criminals then simply mug their victim, demanding any money which the victim obtains.

3. The criminals may distract the victim while the victim has the card in his hand, steal it, and then demand the PIN. Some victims write their PIN on the card, saving the criminals this necessity. If not, the criminals may demand the PIN after intimidating the victim.

4. If the thieves are not in a hurry, they may demand that the victim withdraw more money from the bank account. They may also demand the victim's card, PIN and any cash which the victim has, perhaps threatening him with a knife or even a gun.

While likely to be effective at getting some money from the victim, this scam is less effective than the more sophisticated rip-offs covered in scam #23 because the victim knows that he has been robbed. Unless he has been killed or seriously injured, the victim will be able to report the theft and cancel the card before the account has been looted to any great extent, since almost all bank accounts have strict limits on the amounts that can be withdrawn from ATMs each day. Unless the victim is on a very tight budget, or even if he is, the greatest damage from these and similar crimes is therefore often the trauma from which the victims suffered from being mugged.

To get around the daily withdrawal limits on ATM cards, criminals prefer to operate around 11:30 or 11:45 in the evening. Not only will it be dark, but they can then withdraw twice the maximum daily amount – one maximum just before midnight, and one just after, before the card is cancelled. If the victim's bank is on a different time zone from the criminals, however, it might frustrate this trick, since midnight to the home bank will be at a different time from midnight to the criminals.

Many police departments issue advice on how to avoid being mugged at ATMs. While the advice can differ in detail, there are a number of common features:

- It is usually best to use ATMs inside buildings such as banks during business hours, if possible, or stores, if not. Thieves will prefer to mug customers at ATMs on a street, especially as ATMs inside banks often have surveillance cameras.

- Have your ATM or credit card ready and in your hand as you approach the ATM, as the act of searching for it and getting it out can distract you. Do not wait to get to the ATM to take your card out of your pocket, wallet or purse.

- In all but the safest areas, try and be aware of your surroundings and those around you at all times.

- It is best not to count money at the ATM, unless you are in a busy, secure area such as a bank, as outdoor ATMs are such a magnet for muggers. If you have not got the correct amount of money from the machine, there is, in any case, nothing you can do to correct the mistake at the ATM there and then.

- As a general rule, it is better to avoid taking out money at night, but if it is unavoidable, it is much better to stick to busy, well-lit areas, while taking precautions to avoid pickpockets or people spying on your hand as it enters the PIN. Thieves can wait to ambush customers while they finish their business at ATMs, and it can be better to select another ATM if there are lots of trees or shrubbery or other convenient places for thieves to hide nearby.

- If anyone follows you after you have taken money from an ATM, particularly at night, go to the nearest busy, well-lit area, and if they keep following you, call the police. It is probably better for women not to go alone to ATMs at night anywhere with a bad reputation for street crime – if they need cash urgently, they should consider taking a companion.

35-year-old Belgian tourist kidnapped in India after using an ATM

A Belgian tourist was travelling from Ahmedabad, India to Bombay. He withdrew 10,000 rupees ($125/£100) from an ATM on the platform of Kalupur railway station. He was then approached by three thugs who pretended to sell him foreign merchandise. They picked up his bags and moved to a tuk-tuk. He followed them and was forced into the vehicle. The thugs then beat him up and dumped his body miles away, having stolen his credit cards, money, travellers' cheques and passport. He did not file a report with the police.

A few days later, however, the police were working on a different case and became suspicious of the tuk-tuk. They followed it, stopped it and searched it. They found the Belgian's passport, credit cards and cash. The men claimed to have found the stolen property near the station, but later confessed to having robbed the tourist.

23. "We've got your wallet at the police station" scam

Likely damage: 3/5

Frequency: 2/5

Countries reported: South America.

Summary: Scammers steal the tourist's wallet, and then call him twice, trying to acquire his PIN.

This scam is yet another way for scammers to get hold of their victims' ATM or debit cards and the associated PINs. It is rather ingenious, but requires organisation and some risk on the part of the scammers, and so will probably never be as widespread as simply holding people up at ATMs, demanding that they withdraw money and then stealing it (see scam #22). It has been reported in particular from Latin America.

It works as follows:

1. The scammers mug the victim, or pick his pocket, and steal his wallet. A good pickpocket may steal several in one night.

2. The victim's ATM, credit and debit cards are taken. The thieves are not, however, interested in using the cards in the usual way, to buy lots of easily marketable goods. They want cash, which is much more difficult to trace, so they need PINs for each of the cards, so that they can use them at ATMs.

3. After robbing the victim, the thieves follow him, note the hotel he is staying at, and then call him twice, asking for his room using his name, which will be on the cards they have kept.

4. In the first call, the scammers will pretend to be an English-speaking officer at the local police station. The scammers will say that the victim's wallet and cards have been found, and the victim will be asked to go to the police station to retrieve his items and fill in a police report.

5. The scammers will give the victim an address, which they will claim is the address of the police station, but which will probably turn out to be non-existent (though there have been cases of fake police stations being set up to scam tourists).

6. Relieved, the victim will prepare to leave his hotel and look for it. Shortly afterwards, he will get a second call from the scammers. He may still be at his hotel, or he may have left it if the scammers can reach him on a mobile phone. This time, the scammers will pretend to be from the victim's bank or credit card company, and will say that the local police have told them that he has been robbed. They will say that they will be glad to cancel his credit cards, but first they need information. Could he please confirm his name, address, date of birth, mother's maiden name and PIN or PINs if there is more than one card? The PINs are, of course, what they want.

7. A trusting customer who is probably distracted and trying to find a non-existent address will give the crooks his PIN, and his bank and credit card accounts can then be looted. Because he thinks that he has cancelled his cards, he will probably not call his bank or credit card company again, and the first he knows of the theft may well be when he receives the bills when he returns home.

If the scammers have overdrawn their victim's account, his credit can be ruined and he can face big bills for interest from his banks and credit card companies. Repairing the damage from this or similar scams can take months or years and is often extremely stressful.

Some ways to avoid becoming a victim of this scam are:

- To be extremely suspicious if you receive an unsolicited call from your bank while you are travelling, and *never* give your PIN out to your bank over the phone, no matter how plausible the person who pretends to be from your bank seems to be. No reputable bank ever asks for your PIN in full (though they occasionally ask for the last two digits) and being asked for it, whether over the phone or online, is a sure sign that you are about to be scammed.

- To be aware that even automated services may be controlled by scammers. Sometimes, the thieves will pretend to put you through to an automated service which takes your PIN for you. In fact, the "automated service" is a recording device which they control and which will actually be recording the numbers you tap in, so giving the scammers your PIN without you actually telling them what it is.

- Perhaps the best way to avoid this scam, however, is to hang up when somebody saying that they are from your bank calls you and call them back at a number which you already know is controlled by your bank, or a number which you can find on the bank's website.

---

24. Currency exchange scams

Likely damage: 2/5

Frequency: 3/5

Countries reported: Global.

Summary: How people who offer to change travellers' cash into the local currency can scam their customers.

Most people who travel internationally will have to change money at some point, unless they manage to stay in countries which use the same currency as they do at home. Currencies used in several countries include the euro, the West African CFA franc or the US dollar. In many poorer countries, there is no realistic alternative to using money changers, either because there are no ATMs, or because most of the ATMs only take local cards. Even if a tourist uses ATMs everywhere to take money out of his bank account, at some point she is likely to need to change money on the street or in a bank, either because she has run out of cash, or because she wants to get rid of some of the local currency, before she leaves. It may also be that she thinks she can get a better rate from the street traders.

With the exception of taxi-driving (see scams #9, #13 and #14), few, if any, activities connected to travelling are subject to more rip-offs than the process of exchanging cash in one currency for cash in another. Many street money-changers may be honest people trying to make a living, but enough are dishonest to make their profession notorious for swindling travellers. It is a very attractive business for small scale criminals because it does not require any start-up capital or equipment, except a calculator. It also involves large amounts of cash, and because tourists are often on the move when they change money, they often cannot complain to the police, even if they subsequently discover that they have been conned.

Most of the scams are widespread and fairly simple. One scam related to buying foreign currency involves a "money-changer" and "undercover policemen", and is covered in scam #58. Another typical con runs as follows:

1. A traveller wants to change a fairly substantial amount of money. He hands it over to a money-changer.

2. The money-changer may attempt to slip old and worthless notes or even newspaper cuttings into the wad of local currency which he hands over to the traveller.

3. As the wad of local currency is fairly big, the traveller may not notice the deception until he tries to spend the money and the banknote is rejected.

4. If the traveller does notice the trick somehow, the money-changer can simply apologise and hand over a genuine note, and will have lost nothing.

Another trick for money changers to swindle their customers is to take advantage of many people's poor mental arithmetic. This is even easier to do in situations when the victim is in a hurry to catch a flight or a bus or can be distracted in some way, as multiplying numbers is even more difficult when people's minds are on something else. In transactions involving currencies with many zeroes, for example, they may lose one, meaning that the victim's $100 bill has bought him $10 of the local currency (see scam #21). Again, if the scammer is challenged, he can simply rectify the mistake, and will have lost nothing. Alternatively, he can deny that his victim has handed him a $100 bill, and because the transaction was in cash and was probably not witnessed, he can probably get away with it.

Money changers have even been known to trick travellers by manipulating their calculators:

1. The scamming moneychanger swaps the rubber or plastic buttons "=" and "MR" on the keypad.

2. He then saves a random, but low, number in the calculator's memory – perhaps the equivalent of $30/£25 in the local currency – say, 300,000, at an exchange rate of 10,000 to the dollar.

3. When a tourist asks him to change $100 or $200, he can enter the number "100" or "200" in the calculator, and enter the correct exchange rate. He then presses the button with the "=" sign on it, which is actually the "MR" button.

4. The number which he had saved is then displayed – 300,000, which is the equivalent of $30, rather than 1,000,000 or 2,000,000, which is what $100 or $200 is worth.

5. He gives the tourist 300,000 of the foreign currency, and walks away perhaps $100 richer.

Finally, in this section, a dishonourable mention is due to currency exchanges in airports. In my experience, these almost always have by far the worst rates of any legitimate currency exchanges in their cities (with the possible exception of hotels, see scam #7), and many of them charge very high commissions. When a traveller arrives at a foreign airport and clears customs and immigration, the first sight he sees is often one of these kiosks, and because he may need money for a taxi or the airport bus, he feels obliged to use them. The airport will often give the currency exchange this good spot because they can make money out of it, either by owning the currency exchange directly or, more usually, by charging it a high rent. In my experience, the ATMs which are likely to offer the traveller a much better exchange rate (but from which the airport makes much less money) are usually located beyond the currency exchange, and often hidden somewhat out of the way. I have often had to ask for directions to find an ATM at any airport, but it has always been completely obvious, where the currency exchange is.

To avoid scams involving currency exchanges it is far better to change money at reputable-looking banks, or withdraw money using ATM cards, rather than using currency dealers on the street. As mentioned above, however, it is not always possible to do this, particularly in poorer countries.

Ways to avoid scams involving street currency exchanges include:

- Always know exactly what the exchange rate in the country to which you are travelling is. Calculate how much of the local currency you expect for your home currency.

- Count any notes you are given, and if possible have a witness, such as a travelling companion, for each transaction. Have no hesitation in rejecting notes which are badly damaged or torn, or do not look like others of a similar value.

My experience of a money-changing scam on the El Salvador-Guatemala border

I encountered another common scam at the border between El Salvador and Guatemala. There were no banks or ATMs at the border where I crossed, and arriving in a country without any of the local currency is always slightly worrying. Since most travellers have no idea what the exchange rate is between the US dollar (which El Salvador uses) and the Guatemalan quetzal, some of the money changers, including the one I used, stated a highly misleading exchange rate at first, offering me two hundred quetzals for $50, or a rate of 4:1, rather than four hundred quetzals, or 8:1, which was the exchange rate at the time. I was just about to hand over the money when I thought better of it, asked another traveller what the exchange rate should be, and demanded a much better rate, which I got without further argument. The money changer had lost nothing by attempting to scam me, and the $25 which he could have gained from his two-minute scam was more than most honest people in Guatemala earn in a day.

Chapter 4: Travel agent and travel club scams

Most people who travel at all have used travel agents. Some offer good and convenient deals at low prices. However, as with any business, and perhaps more than most, many travel agents are fraudulent, selling customers products which are fake, or worthless, and disappearing with their money. These businesses can ruin holidays and even lives, as well as swindling their victims out of large sums of money.

Most travel agents are classic middlemen, selling products and taking a commission or fee for doing so. Like most middlemen, it is often in their interests to exaggerate the merits of their product. They will sell more that way, so make more in fees, and they will probably not be held responsible when the tour or bus journey does not live up to the customer's expectations. Either the customer will be somewhere else, or he or she will blame the tour company in the first instance.

Travel clubs, like timeshare sales businesses, are very often fraudulent. Many use high pressure sales pitches to force customers to sign up. The scammers amongst them pretend to offer their customers cheap vacations in exchange for one-off or annual fees, but then offer them deals which they could have got anyway, online or otherwise. They often make it very difficult to opt out of their clubs once the victim has been lured in.

25. Lying travel agent scams

Likely damage: 2/5

Frequency: 4/5

Countries reported: Global.

Summary: Travel agents scam tourists by selling them tours which are unsafe or bus journeys which take much longer than they say they will.

There is an old joke about lawyers and politicians. Q: How do you know a lawyer/politician is lying? A: His lips are moving.

Many travel agents lie. They lie repeatedly, they lie casually, and they lie convincingly. They then, of course, deny that they have lied even when their customers catch them out. Their motive for lying is obvious: they want their victims to buy something from them and the better they can make it sound, the more likely their victims are to buy it. If their victim is buying a ticket to another city, and is obviously on a tour, they can assume that their victim is unlikely to return so will be most unlikely to complain about their lies. The most their victim will do is post something on a website warning other travellers about his experience, or send an e-mail to any of his friends who are likely to buy a similar product from the same travel agent.

After being scammed by travel agents repeatedly, I worked out that it was better to allow for their lies and assume that my bus journeys would end much later than they told me they would (see example below), or that my tours would not be as good. This often does not matter particularly – in a one month or two month trip, an extra couple of hours staring out of a bus window is no disaster. Rarely, it can even be good: if the traveller's hotel has a time before which he or she is not allowed to check in, a bus which arrives two hours late can save him two hours of wandering around the city with bags. Often, however, it can mean a missed travel connection or a missed appointment. I have known people to miss flights home because their buses took far more time than the travel agent said they would.

Bus rides are an easily quantifiable example of people being scammed by travel agents. Travel agents scam travellers in many other ways, however, and many of them are more serious. I remember being sold a four-day tour of a desert in South America which promised three-star accommodation and three meals per day. The hotels we stayed in were mostly one-star, or even worse, and we had to buy our own dinners. Of course we complained, but were out in the middle of nowhere, and were effectively told to shut up, or we would have to walk home. We chose to be cowardly and kept quiet.

I have seen agencies offering diving or climbing tours who advertise "your safety is our priority", but who rent obviously unsafe equipment to their customers. Needless to say, it is best to check any equipment to which you plan to entrust your life, and steer as far away as possible from businesses which do not let you, or whose equipment is substandard. Some agencies in my experience have tried to sell me a bus or plane ticket, telling me that no other bus company or airline covered the route in question. I found out subsequently that this was not true. I have had travel agents tell me that a particular attraction can only be seen as part of a tour, only to find out that there was a public bus that dropped me just outside.

I should also say that travel agents have often sold me tours or bus or plane tickets at a reasonable price which turned out to be broadly as they described them. Occasionally, I have been very grateful to them for saving me lots of money and trouble. Once, in Lima, Peru, I needed to book a one-way flight at short notice to Sao Paulo, Brazil, to catch my plane home. All the quotes I had seen online were $500 (then £300) or more. I went to a travel agent around the corner from my hotel and she found me a flight for $240/£150. Needless to say, I was very glad that I had shopped around.

It is impossible to avoid travel agents or tour operators who lie, but to try to minimize the damage, I recommend the following:

- It is best to treat all travel agents' claims as exaggerated, even more than with any other form of commercial advertising. Do not forget that they are salesman whose weekly wage may well depend on selling you that tour. They know vastly more about the business than you do, and they will also know that few tourists complain, and even fewer complain successfully.

- If possible, use a travel agency recommended by friends or relatives.

- In particular, as advised above, ask to check any equipment, such as diving or climbing gear, which you will be trusting with your life – if the agency refuses, do not deal with them.

Expedia delayed my refund by six months, 2014-5

In 2014, I booked a trip to Ethiopia with the large web travel agent, Expedia, to see that country's northern historical circuit for a couple of weeks. At the airport, however, I heard that the plane had developed a fault and the flight was cancelled. The contrast between the reactions of Ethiopian Airlines and Expedia was remarkable. Ethiopian paid me compensation. They also paid for my 3 a.m. taxi back from the airport.

Expedia, however, invented every excuse imaginable to delay refunding my ticket so that I could rebook it for the following year. Months and months of furious late night phone calls to their call centre got me nowhere, and Expedia are not in ABTA, so there was no industry association to which I could complain. Finally, I read online that complaining to a newspaper was the only way to get the money back in these cases, so I wrote to the Guardian's and the New York Times's travel sections. Ten days later, I got my refund. Judging by a quick online search, I am one of very many who has been treated this way by Expedia. I still use their website for comparing prices, but will never book through them again.

Friends scammed by a travel agent in Sydney, Australia

A few years ago, I was staying in Sydney. Some friends booked a tour around Sydney Harbour to see the fireworks for Australia

Day. They were promised a luxury cruise, an excellent view and first-class food. The boat turned out to be a patched-up old tub which gave off diesel fumes; they had no view of the fireworks because they were on the wrong side of the boat and by the time it had turned, the fireworks were over; and the food was inedible. They wasted their money and their time.

Travel agents lying about bus journeys

During one of my overseas trips, I started keeping a list of the times that travel agents told me that a bus journey would take, and the actual time it took. I kept it up when I travelled subsequently, and it now covers about 20 bus rides. I have deliberately excluded journeys where I remember that we were significantly delayed because of a problem outside the bus driver's control, for example a car crash or unexpected snowfall. Here are some typical entries:

Promised and actual length of bus journeys

Thailand - Bangkok to Ko Chang (inc. ferry)

- Duration of bus journey according to travel agent: 5 hours

- Actual duration of bus journey: 7 hours

Chile/Bolivia - San Pedro de Atacama to Uyuni

- Duration of bus journey according to travel agent: 10 hours

- Actual duration of bus journey: 11.5 hours

Bolivia - Uyuni to La Paz

- Duration of bus journey according to travel agent: 11 hours

- Actual duration of bus journey: 13.5 hours

Guatemala - Lanquin to Flores

- Duration of bus journey according to travel agent: 6-7 hours

- Actual duration of bus journey: 9 hours

United States – Sacramento to Reno

- Duration of bus journey according to travel agent: 3.5 hours

- Actual duration of bus journey: 5 hours

Note: the American bus journey was sold to me by the bus company, rather than by a travel agent.

None of the bus rides for which I bought tickets took less time than I was told by the travel agent that they would, and most took significantly longer – a quarter or a fifth longer.

26. Fraudulent travel agent scams

Likely damage: 4/5

Frequency: 2/5

Countries reported: Global.

Summary: Travel agents who scam tourists by taking their money and running, or pretending that they have won prize holidays and getting them to call premium rate phone numbers.

There is a difference between travel agents who exaggerate the merits of whatever they are trying to sell their customers (covered in scam #25), and those who take their customers' money without the slightest intention of giving them any product in return. One clearly blends into the other, and both practices are illegal in most countries. Also semi-criminal are travel agents who intend to supply their customers with something that is completely unrecognisable from what they led them to expect they were buying. However, most people would agree that disappearing with customers' money without giving them anything in return is a much more serious form of fraud than overselling a product.

Fraudulent travel agencies have been around for as long as genuine travel agencies have existed. There are any number of ways in which travellers can be defrauded. Most are not particularly subtle or complicated, involving selling victims a tour or plane ticket, and then trying to disappear with the money.

The Internet has opened up lots of new ways for fraudulent travel agencies to swindle their unsuspecting customers. Fraudulent travel agencies use spam and fake websites to lure customers into handing over their cash (see scams #49 and #51). Their spam can be quite difficult to distinguish from advertising by genuine travel agencies. A typical rip-off works as follows:

1. The scammers send e-mails saying that the victim has won a dream holiday or cruise. To claim, the victim has to call a premium rate phone number.

2. The victim calls, but is put on hold, all the while racking up expensive phone charges.

3. He is then subjected to a long sales pitch. If he has not already hung up, he is asked to give his credit card information for the holiday.

4. His card is charged, probably for far more than he agreed to pay.

5. The tickets for the holiday never arrive.

The same tips which apply to avoiding fake travel agencies in newspapers apply to agencies which advertise using e-mails.

To avoid this kind of fraud:

- It is better to pay for package holidays or airline tickets with a credit card. Dealing with a company that only accepts cash for large items is very risky. In most countries, credit card companies will refund their customers if they are victims of fraud, though the exact conditions vary from country to country.

- If you are suspicious about a transaction, raise a query with your credit card company as early as possible.

- Ensure that any travel agent you are dealing with is accredited and registered with the relevant authorities or industry organisations. Almost all reputable travel agents in America are registered with one or more industry organisations such as ASTA (the American Society of Travel Agents), USTOA (the United States Tour Operators Association), IATAN (the International Airline Travel Agency Network) or the BBB (the Better Business Bureau). In California, for example, they should also be accredited with the state Attorney General's Office (which has a useful list at http://ag.ca.gov/travel/). In Britain, they should be registered with the Association of British Travel Agents (ABTA).

- Check out the company online to ensure that there are no fraud complaints associated with it. Searching for the company's name online with "scam" or "fraud" after it is surprisingly effective in finding companies which have swindled customers in the past.

- Try and find friends or family who have dealt with the company in the past for booking travel. Personal recommendations from people you trust are often the best way to find reliable travel agents.

- As so often, if a deal looks too good to be true, it probably is.

- If you have an electronic ticket for a flight, call the airline and ask for an aisle or window seat. This will make them check that your reservation exists, and that you have not paid money for a ticket that was never booked with the airline. Few airlines, mostly in less developed countries, still offer paper tickets, but if you buy such a ticket issued by a travel agent, ensure that the Status box on the ticket is marked "OK" or "HK".

British Muslim tourists ripped off by fraudulent travel agent

A travel agent sold tours to 300 British Muslims who wanted to make the annual Haj pilgrimage to Mecca. The packages cost up to £2,000/$2,500 and many of the pilgrims had saved for several years to be able to go on the journey which Muslims are supposed to do at least once in their lives. The agent, Mohammed Ahmed, received and pocketed the money, and the tours did not take place. He was sentenced to six years in prison.

Fake British travel agent convicted in bizarre revenge scam

In 2016, Kay Hooper was convicted of posing as a travel agent and swindling customers out of £56,000/$67,000. Bizarrely, she did so to get revenge on **a company who cut her holiday short because she lost her passport.** She set up the fake business, called Travel Connections, from Great Torrington, Devon, after filling in an online form. She had planned to continue the scam and had booked 54 cruises costing more than £300,000 through 2016 and into 2017.

The company realised what was going on after they noticed she had personally taken eight cruises in six months. Kay Hooper admitted fraud and was sentenced to 20 months in prison suspended for two years, given a six-month curfew and ordered to pay a £100 victim surcharge by Recorder Timothy Rose at Exeter Crown Court.

Florida Attorney General's office closes down travel club scams

Fraudulent travel clubs are a rapidly growing scam. It is easy to find the names of the worst on websites such as Complaints.com. They usually advertise either through spam on the Internet or with classified ads in newspapers. They target a large, but vulnerable, group of people; those who want a cheap vacation somewhere for themselves and their family, but do not have the time or the inclination to check out the people selling them the trip. The clubs will demand a membership fee, generally of thousands of dollars, pounds or euros. In exchange, their members will be offered deals which seem almost too good to be true, and usually are.

In December 2015, the Florida Attorney General's office closed down three travel clubs which, it claimed, had been deceiving the public. The clubs had:

- Charged for items advertised as free

- Sold vacation packages that could not be used because of burdensome blackout dates and overly restrictive terms and conditions

- Refused to provide refunds or allow cancellation of purchases

- Greatly exaggerated savings

- Made unauthorized charges to consumer credit cards.

The following month, it closed down several more, including Reservation Services International, Map Destinations, LLC and Florida Beaches Destinations Club, LLC. The office said that the companies had employed "unscrupulous sales tactics to induce consumers into purchasing vacation club memberships".

27. Visa-related scams

Likely damage: 2/5

Frequency: 3/5

Countries reported: Global.

Summary: Scammers target travellers by pretending they can get visas when they cannot, or charging far too much when they can.

Worth being noted as a scam in itself is the possibility of being charged too much by travel agents or other third parties for visas to visit countries which require you to have a visa to visit. Most people who travel for fun are from wealthy countries in North America, Europe, East Asia or Australia, and most of those countries do not require citizens of other wealthy countries to obtain visas before they visit. (Dishonourable exceptions to this are Australia, which charges Americans and Europeans A$20 ($15/£13) for the right to visit, and the United States, which charges $14 for the same). This is, therefore, a scam which mostly affects either travellers from wealthy countries visiting poorer countries, or the citizens of poorer countries travelling anywhere. Travellers often require a visa if they are on an extended visit to other rich countries, or intend to work there, even if they would not normally require a visa to visit for a shorter length of time.

Closely related to this scam is the swindle which offers to organise visas for travellers, and simply takes their money and gives them a worthless stamp or piece of paper in exchange. This rip-off may affect people from anywhere in the world who seek to buy a visa, though thieves tend to target countries, such as the United States, Britain and the Schengen group, whose visas are particularly in demand. See the example below for a description of a variant of this scam in Thailand.

A large number of scammers target citizens of poorer countries trying to obtain work or tourism visas for Europe or the United States. These scams are so widespread that many embassies warn against them. Some scammers offer to supply forged documents to assist with visa applications. The forgeries they provide are often low quality and easily detected by the immigration officials whom they attempt to deceive. Scammers may even offer fake visas for a fee, though only a country's government can issue genuine visas. These scammers can be reported to www.econsumer.gov, a website set up by consumer protection groups from seventeen countries which targets international scammers.

Another scam is to pretend that travellers need to go through the criminal's website to obtain a legitimate visa, when in fact the visa is free from the country's embassy or online (see the example below for a description of this type of fraud in relation to the American government's ESTA). I have also heard many stories of immigration officials trying to scam tourists using visa rules, some of which are in the last example (see below).

To avoid being charged an excessive amount for a visa by a travel agent

- Check how much the visa will cost the travel agent to obtain. All countries list visa fees on an official website, usually of the embassy in question or their foreign affairs ministry.

- If the travel agent has to fill in forms for you, take your passport over to the embassy and bring it back to the agency, it is clearly legitimate for them to ask for a fee in excess of what they must pay the country whose visa you are buying.

- However, if the charge seems at all excessive, do not deal with the travel agent unless you have no choice. Agents who swindle travellers in this way may well have no scruples about raising the price yet further once they have your passport, or selling passport information to criminal gangs.

Visa fraud in Thailand

An example of this type of scam targets travellers in Thailand. European tourists are given a visa valid for 30 days on arrival in Thailand. Travel agencies on the Khao Sanh Road in Bangkok have sold tourists fake stamps which are supposed to extend their visas. However, these stamps are, in fact, worthless, and British and Dutch tourists have been arrested trying to leave Thailand after their visas had expired. If convicted of staying in Thailand illegally, the victims could face prison sentences of up to ten years. According to the Thai government, the only places to obtain visa extensions are from Thai government offices. Visa extensions obtained elsewhere are probably fraudulent.

Electronic System for Travel Authorisation fraud

In 2008, the United States introduced its Electronic System for Travel Authorisation (ESTA), which required foreigners who qualified for the Visa Waiver program to register online 48 hours before visiting the United States. The registration is free, takes about two minutes to complete and is valid for two years. However, websites sprang up almost immediately demanding fees of $30/£20-$100/£60 per person to apply for ESTAs on their behalf. Once the fee had been paid, they would direct tourists to the US government website. US embassies in countries whose citizens were covered by the Visa Waiver program received many calls from people who had been tricked in this way. Their advice was that the ESTA was free and easily obtainable online from the US government, whose websites ended in ".gov".

Examples of crooked border officials

At the border between Thailand and Cambodia, for example, at Poipet or Koh Kong, Cambodian immigration officials often demand 100-300 Thai Baht ($3/£2.50-$9/£8) extra from tourists for Cambodian visas. They may also try to persuade tourists to pay 100 Baht for the entry or exit stamps, which are, in fact, free.

In Tanzania, many travellers have been approached by "immigration officials" who identified problems with their visas, which were, in fact, in order. Needless to say, the "officials" demanded "on-the-spot fines" as an alternative to going to jail. Occasionally, corruption can work in a traveller's favour. Arriving at Caracas airport in Venezuela, an acquaintance of mine, whose papers were definitely not in order, bribed the immigration officials $500 for authentic passport stamps and was able to avoid being put in jail and deported immediately.

Crossing many African borders overland, officials will pretend that your visa is not in order, and will require a "fee" to sort the difficulty out. If you know the rules, and demand to speak to the guard's superior, you may not have to pay the fee. On the other hand, you are likely to find that the superior is mysteriously unavailable, or else that the superior demands an additional fee on top of what you were asked for originally.

28. "Volunteering" scams

Likely damage: 4/5

Frequency: 2/5

Countries reported: Global, particularly in countries where there is a strong tradition of volunteering and little effective oversight.

Summary: Travellers who volunteer to help in development projects in developing countries find their advance fees stolen, or are exploited once they start work.

Volunteering to help with development projects or social work in foreign countries is a rapidly growing industry, particularly in Latin America, Africa and South Asia. It is thought to be worth £1.5 billion/$2 billion per year. Tens of thousands of travellers every year spend all or part of their time overseas helping the countries in which they travel. Most find the opportunity to be involved with local people and to help the local environment a pleasure, even a privilege.

There are a large number of reputable organisations which specialise in matching travellers with opportunities to volunteer. Many of these organisations charge application and other fees, to cover their own costs.

Inevitably, however, scammers have realised that, since foreigners are willing to pay to volunteer, there are significant opportunities for scamming. The usual way in which people volunteer presents several opportunities to steal, giving little or nothing in return. The first chance occurs before the victims leave home, while they are researching the possibilities for volunteering overseas. Some unscrupulous scammers set up fake organisations which take potential volunteers' money and then simply fail to arrange any volunteering jobs when they arrive in the foreign country. They will advertise from the country in which the supposed volunteer job is located, claiming to "cut out the middleman", and asking "why pay more for volunteering? Pay us directly instead and save". They will give the name of a genuine project which the victim can check out. When she arrives in the country, however, having spent her money on an air fare, there will be no-one to meet her. If the victim travels to the site at her own expense, she will find that nobody has heard of her, and there is no work for her to do. The address of the organisation with whom she has booked will be fake. Any inquiries by phone or email lead to dead ends. This is one of the "advance-fee fraud" scam family. Of course, the project at which she arrives might well be able to use her services anyway, but there is no guarantee of this, and she will have lost the money she paid in fees to the fake organisation.

In many cases, legitimate travel agents see volunteers as just another group of tourists and offer them "volunteering" holidays similar to their "trekking" and "adventure" tours. Such holidays are unlikely to be of any benefit to the country which the victim is visiting. They are designed for the travel agent's profit. Volunteering holidays can often be distinguished from charitable volunteering in two ways: the travel agent asks for lots of up-front fees, and the destinations where the "volunteering" takes place can be remarkably similar to those on the "trekking" and "adventure" tours.

Even legitimate organisations which do arrange placements sometimes charge excessive fees. Often, the money goes to the organisation's owners in large profit margins, but it can also go into plush offices and expensive marketing efforts and brochures.

It can be interesting to ask charities how much of the fees you are contributing goes into their overheads, and how much is spent directly on charitable projects. In some countries, there is a law stating the maximum proportion of income which can spent on overheads and still be consistent with charitable status, though in many other countries, either there is no maximum, or it is not enforced.

Volunteers can also be scammed once they have arrived at their project and have started work. In Hanoi, I met a young Australian who had gone to Vietnam to teach English. He told me that he had fallen out with the management of the school because they had refused to pay him as much as they had promised. They had kept his passport at the start of his assignment and he had had to work as an unpaid slave until he had seen an opportunity to steal it back. I have met more than one person who has arrived at a project and was told that there was no work for them to do. They had to go home at their own expense.

In order to avoid being swindled while volunteering your time:

- It is important to research the organisation which you are using. Check for membership of industry organisations, and search for reviews online to find out how many of its customers are satisfied.

- You can also call the organisation and ask for contact details for previous volunteers to obtain their feedback.

- Ensure that you pin down exactly what you will be doing, what the organisation will pay for, as well as what you yourself will be expected to pay for.

- Assume that you will have to pay for anything that is not specifically covered.

- Do not trust any organisations which demand money straight away; most legitimate organisations will want to make sure that you are motivated and dedicated enough to be an asset to their project before you pay anything.

Volunteering scams in Nepal

Many foreigners who volunteered in Nepal were short-changed in various ways, according to an article in the Nepali Times in 2012. One American man said that, despite paying an upfront fee, his host family did not receive the money they had been promised for his accommodation. This quickly poisoned the mood in the village against him. In another incident, a large group of Polish volunteers paid an NGO in advance for bulk food supplies for an orphanage, which never arrived.

---

29. Tour guide scams

Likely damage: 2/5

Frequency: 1/5

Countries reported: Global.

Summary: How substandard or fraudulent tour guides can exploit and rob tourists.

Expensive tourist guides are compulsory for independent travellers in a few countries (see scam #46). That is a government scam, not a swindle by the guides themselves. Guides or porters are often necessary for travellers who want to get off the beaten path. A good guide can show tourists places they would not otherwise find, and tell them information about sights which they would not otherwise be told. This section of the book, however, is about the nine most common ways in which guides scam tourists.

First, when tourists plan their treks in a national park, guides will often tell you that their services are compulsory when they are not. Guides can thereby persuade tourists to hire them, when they would not otherwise be able to. This scam is relatively easy for the swindler because the tourists may not be familiar with the regulations in the foreign national park. This scam is most common in national parks in poor countries.

Second, the guides will tell their victims that they know the area which their victims are visiting and its wildlife or history well when they do not. Most of the guides I have hired have given their customers fascinating tours. Others, however, have simply regurgitated what I have read in my guidebook or found online with no difficulty. Some countries regulate tourist guides, but many others do not, and even where regulations exist, such as in South Africa, they are not always enforced. In those countries, the government often cracks down to try to control unlicensed tourist guides, but that they have to do so regularly indicates that these guides still operate.

Third, fraudulent guides often pretend that they speak English when they speak it badly. They often speak rapidly, with a strong foreign accent and relate information which they have learned by heart. Even straining to understand, they can be difficult to follow, and over background noise or from the back of a tour party, virtually impossible. I have been on tours where the guide tried to explain the history of a monument or the biology of an animal species but nobody in the party could understand what he was saying. Guides like this are a complete waste of money.

Fourth, tour guides sometimes lead their customers to destinations to which they do not want to go (see the example below about tours in China). As has been mentioned in many other sections of this book, restaurants or shops will often give guides commissions if they bring tourists to the business, and if the tourists buy something. The commission will be added to the tourists' bills. This is not necessarily bad; some tourists want to buy souvenirs, and being taken to shops by their guides is a quick way to find what they want. However, if travellers have no interest in shopping, or are on a tight schedule, seeing jewellery or jade shops is not necessarily how they want to spend their tour.

Fifth, guides have been known to attack and rob tourists directly (see example below). As the travellers are paying their guide to allow them to follow him, it is often relatively easily for him to take them to an isolated spot and rob them. See the second example below.

Sixth, many guides ask aggressively for tips once they have done their job. They often simply start talking to tourists, and lead them on hour-long tours, without mentioning that they expect to be paid for their services at the end. It is easy enough, therefore, for travellers to believe that a nice man is showing them around for nothing. At the end of their tour, however, the guide will always ask the tourists for money. The guide is taking a risk that they will refuse to pay, but this cannot happen often, otherwise the guide would always demand money up front.

Seventh, some guides rob tourists by leading them to an isolated part of the desert or mountains and refusing to take them back to safety unless they are paid. This form of extortion is rare, but has been known to happen. It only works on long hikes where the party is in a deserted area and no help is to be expected. It can work particularly well in deserts or jungles where the wildlife is notoriously dangerous; most tourists would pay whatever is necessary to be led out of that sort of danger. See the example below for another variant of this scam.

Eighth, bear in mind that, as with hotels, online reviews for individual tour guides are not always trustworthy. I have heard that some guides write their own reviews and then post them online. Some agencies even advertise in backpacker haunts for travellers to do this for them in English, offering cash or free tours in return.

Ninth, guides sometimes try to demand payment for "extras", particularly on multi-day tours. Tourists sometimes find, during a long trip in a wilderness, that they are expected to pay for the guide's accommodation and food as well as their own. They may also find that they are required to pay for his ticket for parks and attractions. The tourists are often not told about these extras in advance.

To avoid being swindled by a guide:

- It is better to agree a price at the start of a tour than at the end, and to be clear exactly what is included and what is not. I have generally found that I get a worse tour from guides who approach me and who will not leave me alone than guides whom I approach, though this may be only my own experience.

- The best way to find a good guide is probably a personal recommendation from a trusted friend, though this does not guarantee a great experience, or even an honest guide.

Hong Kong guides swindle mainland Chinese tourists

According to the Los Angeles Times, 2015 saw a spate of fraudulent tours in Hong Kong, aimed at mainland Chinese tourists. One of them complained that, as she and two dozen others showed up for the bus to the airport, they were asked for about $50. Over the next four days, she said, her group was compelled to spend hours in a jewellery shop, an electronics dealer, a chocolatier and a cosmetics boutique. At the jewellery shop, she said, she was pressured to spend more than $300 on a necklace charm. Her initial purchase, a $70 bracelet, was rejected by the guide as insufficient to meet her quota.

The same article described the following scam in China. A 26-year-old tourist in Yunnan province chose an expensive tour so as to avoid "forced shopping" but wound up being pressured to buy jewellery and silverware. The tour guide carried a knife, and after she called the tour agency to complain, she said the guide pressed her to withdraw her report.

Illegal tour guides swindle tourists with jade products in China

According to the China Daily, Beijing has many travel agencies whose tour guides seek to scam tourists through offering cut price tours and making their profit through selling them fraudulent "jade" products or traditional medicines. "The cost for a Great Wall-Ming Tombs trip is between 200 yuan ($30/£25) and 240 yuan, but these illegal travel agencies only ask for about 70 yuan", according to a Tourism Bureau official. "For example, they brought those travellers to parts of the Great Wall that do not require a ticket to cut costs. And they only spend two hours in those places and ask travellers to visit jewellery shops or to see doctors for the rest of time".

Fake guide robs Mexican tourist in Bulgaria

In August 2007, a 21-year-old Mexican tourist went on a private tour of the ancient, Thracian tomb in the town of Kazanlak, in central Bulgaria with a guide. The tour also encompassed Tyulbeto Park. The guide mugged the tourist and stole his bag with a credit card, digital camera, documents and personal possessions.

Snake handler extorts money from a tourist in Morocco

Several years ago, my publisher paid a visit to Morocco. In the main square of the historic town of Marrakesh, he was watching one of the famous snake charmers. The snake charmer put a snake around the neck of one of the women watching. She did not look overly comfortable and after a short time, she was done. The snake charmer refused to take the snake away unless she paid him a little extra.

Chapter 5: Shopping scams

For many travellers, shopping is a very important part of a holiday. The souvenirs which people buy should be permanent reminders of good times to themselves, and valued gifts to others. Buying goods which are much cheaper overseas than back home can be as important as buying souvenirs to remind them of the trip.

Tourists are often viewed as relatively soft targets by unscrupulous shop owners, looking to offload expensive junk. Visitors rarely know the local produce well enough to distinguish bad merchandise from good, they tend to be richer than local shoppers in many areas, and they will rarely complain even if they realise they have been ripped off. Scamming tourists is therefore big business for shopkeepers in many parts of the world that get lots of tourists.

30. Fake goods scams

Likely damage: 2/5

Frequency: 5/5

Countries reported: Global.

Summary: Travellers are swindled when souvenirs are not what they seem to be.

If it can be made, it can be faked, and if it has not been faked, that is usually because it is not worth the bother, rather than because counterfeiters have scruples or are afraid of the law. The diversity of counterfeit goods which are targeted at tourists is staggering, for example:

- Fake fur, fake ivory and fake medicines are all big business in many countries, particularly Africa and East Asia.

- Fake IDs are widely available on the Khao Sanh Road in Bangkok.

- I have seen fake Trilobites on sale in Morocco and plastic dinosaur bones in Mongolia.

- Bootlegged CDs and DVDs are on sale throughout the developing world.

- Fake jewellery and counterfeit leather goods grace markets worldwide.

- Fake cigars in Cuba and fake rum in Jamaica can catch the tourist unawares.

I have never been a big souvenir buyer myself. However, like virtually all travellers, I succumb occasionally, buying, for instance, pieces of the notorious Wall in Berlin in 1989. Even for those who have never travelled, or who never buy souvenirs, it does not take much imagination to envisage the hurt which people feel when the jewellery, painting or other trinket turns out to be far inferior to what they thought they were buying. Many souvenirs are, of course, intentionally fake: nobody expects a copy of the Venus de Milo or the Leaning Tower of Pisa, bought for £10/$13 at a market, to be the genuine article, or even a particularly good copy.

There is also a grey area when it comes to bootleg copies of luxury goods such as Chanel handbags or Rolex watches. The firms that make the genuine products undoubtedly suffer from counterfeiting, but a traveller who buys a counterfeit Rolex watch for £25/$30 when the original would cost a hundred times as much can hardly feel cheated!

Nevertheless, goods which are not what their sellers say that they are, are extremely common. If all the pieces of the 'Berlin Wall' sold over the past two decades had been genuine, it would have been long enough to go around the earth, rather than encircling a German city! In many countries, particularly poorer ones, sellers of fake goods target tourists in particular, for the usual reasons that tourists are targeted there.

Though fake souvenirs can turn up anywhere, the problem reached such proportions during the 2008 Beijing Olympics that the Chinese and Hong Kong governments launched several major crackdowns on known manufacturers and retailers of these goods. Pre-emptive action was taken to reduce the counterfeiting of souvenirs for the 2012 London Olympics. These crackdowns are designed to benefit the cities holding the games, not tourists – the Chinese and British governments are desperate to recover as much of the enormous cost of staging the games as possible, and selling overpriced souvenirs is a good way to make money. Counterfeiters do not pay a share of their profits to the city, and often evade sales tax as well, so cities crack down on them.

There are a number of problems which fake goods cause the traveller:

- Local police sometimes target the tourists who buy counterfeit goods, as well as the sellers. Most stories of this type of police raid relate to copies of overpriced fashion, in particular ladies' handbags (see example below). At the very least, fake goods are routinely seized at customs from tourists returning home, though, in most countries, the travellers themselves are not usually prosecuted, unless they are clearly importing goods to resell them. Many law enforcement officials claim, too, that tourists who buy counterfeit goods are funding organised crime and even terrorism.

- Buying counterfeit goods can damage tourists' health as well as their wallets. Fake brand sunglasses, for instance, may well not have the same UV protection as their genuine cousins. They are also unlikely to be shatterproof, so they can shatter into their eyes, and fake toys may conceivably use components which are dangerous to children.

- Being sure that you are buying genuine goods has become more difficult. Many experts in this area have said that counterfeiters have become much more sophisticated. Their goods are more and more difficult to distinguish from genuine products. It used to be easy to distinguish a fake handbag from a real handbag, for instance: the quality of the leather and the stitching were usually worse in fakes than in real bags. Now, it is becoming far more difficult, and even experts can sometimes be fooled.

The three best pieces of advice to avoid buying too many fakes are:

1. To do as much research as possible if you are planning to spend a lot of money.

2. If something looks too good to be true, it probably is. If a good which is commonly faked is on sale absurdly cheap, it is unlikely to be the genuine article. Many people often associate fakes with low quality, and this is often, but not necessarily, the case.

3. It is probably better to expect to be ripped off in this way from time to time while shopping overseas, than to expect to be able to avoid bootlegged goods completely.

Counterfeit goods in Dubai

Dubai is a notorious transit point for counterfeit goods, everything from fake drugs like Viagra – which North Korea also produces – to cigarettes, cosmetics and even spare parts for cars. In 2016, it was estimated the value of counterfeit goods had risen from 16.8 million dirhams (£3.5 million/$4 million) to 34.4 million dirhams (£7.1million/$8.5 million) in the first quarter of this year. Many tourists who shop in Dubai buy such goods, though it is unclear how many consider that the cut-price merchandise they buy is genuine.

Many of the counterfeit goods come from China. Some speculate that North Korea is also involved in counterfeiting.

31. "Native" or "tribal" market scams

Likely damage: 2/5

Frequency: 2/5

Countries reported: Morocco, Indonesia, India, Tunisia.

Summary: Markets which pretend to be authentic and are only organized for tourists.

Many tourists regard buying souvenirs as an important part of their journey. They do not only have to contend with the idea that their souvenir may be fake, however. It is entirely possible, and indeed common in some countries, that the whole market may simply be a show put on for tourists, rather than a traditional native exchange.

I have encountered this scam myself in Morocco (see example below). These fake markets may be a speciality there, but I have heard of them in other parts of the world as well. Of course, fake "native" markets can, in theory, sell genuine goods, just as genuine markets often sell fake goods, but it is far more likely that people willing to go to the trouble of marketing their "market" as native would sell counterfeit goods. Certainly, if my Moroccan experience is anything to go by, any genuine goods in these markets are there either by accident, or because it is not worth the expense of faking them. The organisers had clearly taken the trouble of renting a large room and buying some fake merchandise, and would have expected to get their money back.

Spotting fake tribal markets can be difficult, if they are better disguised than in my Moroccan example. There are some indications which may help to distinguish a fake, from a genuine, market, however:

- Generally speaking, a market is more likely to be genuine if there are locals buying goods at it, rather than just tourists. If it is a fake, only held for the purpose of scamming tourists, then its customers will almost exclusively be foreigners.

- If the market sells goods which are useful to natives, as well as goods that tourists might be interested in, it is probably at least in part a genuine market. For example, a genuine market may sell cheap cloth or plastic alarm clocks, while a tourist market might sell only expensive-looking native clothes and jewellery.

- It is likely, too, though far from certain, that if a guide leads you to a market, it will be a market to some extent set up for tourists, though it may still get some of its business from locals. It may collect a commission for each good that tourists buy from the stallholders.

Fake Berber markets in Morocco

In Fes, the spectacular and almost intact medieval city, some friends and I hired a knowledgeable and otherwise excellent guide who nonetheless seemed to think it his duty to lead us into every carpet and leather store in town. With hindsight, we should have made it clear that we did not want to go shopping. But in any case, at the end of a fascinating day's sightseeing and shopping, he offered to take us to a Berber market. Berbers are the indigenous people of North Africa and the Middle East, somewhat like the Aborigines in Australia or the Native Americans in the Americas. Though many have always been agricultural, they are traditionally thought of as nomadic. As such, their lifestyle and culture are interesting to many tourists.

The visions I had had of a market out in the desert with charming Berbers with whom one would somehow haggle for camels or ceremonial daggers at bargain prices turned out to be wide of the mark. The "market" was in a big room in a modern, concrete building just outside the old town of Fes. The tables held a remarkable display of gaudy trash. Half a dozen other tourists were being led around it by their guides. None were buying any of the overpriced tat on sale. The market was about as traditional and nomadic as I am. We poked around a little, endured the high-pressure salesmanship from the "Berbers" as well as we could, and left as quickly as possible.

Later, I learned that fake Berber markets are fairly common in Morocco. As we managed to spot the fraud immediately, and did not buy anything, I cannot say that the scam was in any way damaging to me or the people I was with. The managers had not bothered to do much to disguise it as Berber at all. Presumably, however, other people had been swindled there, or the markets would not exist (or if it did, its touts would not bother to misrepresent it as a Berber market).

32. Admission ticket scams

Likely damage: 1/5

Frequency: 2/5

Countries reported: Turkey, Egypt, India, Thailand.

Summary: How museum employees steal from tourists while issuing them tickets.

In many countries, foreign tourists may be charged many times what local tourists are charged for exactly the same service at exactly the same tourist attraction. This infuriating, but legal, practice is covered in scam #44. This section is concerned with the ways in which staff at museums or other attractions can supplement their wages by stealing from tourists. Staff at museums are as likely to give tourists the wrong change and pocket the difference as any other badly paid employees. There are a number of ways in which travellers can be swindled, and forced to pay twice for admission to a museum or other tourist attraction. They can also be tricked into paying more than the attraction requires them to pay. While the swindler's take is often very small, being ripped off in this way can ruin a tourist's memory of an otherwise fascinating attraction.

- One unsubtle but effective way in which tourists can be scammed is by overcharging them for the ticket. Ticket prices are usually listed on signs at the box office, but it is easy to scam tourists in countries where Western numerals (1, 2, 3, 4 …) are not used, such as Thailand (๑, ๒, ๓, ๔…). Few tourists can decipher the local script, and therefore the ticket seller can charge whatever he thinks the tourists will pay.

- In attractions where the ticket booth is separate from the admissions barrier, clerks sometimes swindle tourists by simply refusing to issue tickets at all.

In another scam:

1. The tourist stops at the ticket booth and pays her money. She does not realise that the clerk is supposed to issue her a ticket.

2. The clerk gestures to the entrance, and the tourist goes over.

3. The official at the entrance demands a ticket, but the tourist does not have one.

4. She has to go back to the clerk and is made to pay again.

5. In the meantime, the clerk has pocketed her money. If the tourist is in a country where she cannot speak the language, it is difficult for her to complain.

That variant of the scam is not particularly sophisticated. Another way to swindle tourists is slightly more subtle:

1. In many tourist attractions where the booth is separate from the admissions barrier, the ticket issued is in two parts, joined by a dotted or perforated line, like the boarding pass for a flight. The

ticket is torn at the line when the tourist is admitted to the attraction.

2. The ticket booth clerk can sell the tourist a used ticket, which has already been torn.

3. If the victim presents the used ticket at the admissions booth, he will be told that he has to buy another ticket.

4. The ticket booth clerk says that the tourist was trying to gain admission without paying. Sometimes the clerk even threatens to call the police.

Louvre admission ticket scam

In 2013, French police investigated fake tickets presented by Chinese tourists for admission to the great Parisian museum. A criminal gang in China had apparently been producing the passes. Tour parties whose guides were using the fake tickets were thus denied entry into what is normally a highlight of any trip to France. According to CNN, comments on Chinese social media expressed concern about the damage the scam could do to China's image. "Can you please stop forging? This is so embarrassing!" read one post on Weibo, the Chinese equivalent of Twitter.

Admission ticket scam at Armenian tourist attraction in Turkey

Ani is a deserted, medieval Armenian city in Turkey. A thousand years ago, it had a population of 100,000 and was known as the "City of 1,001 Churches". Tourists can visit it for 5 Turkish Lira (about $3/£2). Tickets are printed in two parts. Tourists are often given only one part of the ticket, and could possibly be charged a second time, though more commonly the ticket clerk simply pockets their cash and the Turkish Ministry of Culture gets nothing.

Admission ticket scam at the Pyramids

Three American friends of mine visited the Pyramids of Giza, near Cairo, Egypt. They bought tickets and passed the ticket barrier. They were met by two men in official looking uniforms, who took their tickets again. Without their consent, the three men took them on a tour of the Pyramids, and demanded money from them without handing their tickets back. Since tourists can be asked for their tickets at any time, and can be thrown out if they are not presented, my friends felt obliged to pay.

---

33. Gem/precious stone scams

Likely damage: 4/5

Frequency: 2/5

Countries reported: India, Thailand.

Summary: Famous in Thailand and India. A scammer sells a tourist gems cheaply. The gems turn out to be worthless paste.

This is another old family of rip-offs which can be seriously bad for your wallet. It preys on the greed which so much of us feel – the feeling that with one deal, involving a few hours' work, we can make more money than we would be able to make with weeks or months of drudgery in an office or factory. Though this particular scam may seem so obvious that nobody should fall for it, it still claims many new victims each year.

It has countless variants, but many go something like this:

1. A traveller meets an apparently friendly local, who is in fact looking to scam him, on the street or in a bar in a foreign town.

2. The scammer chats his victim up, perhaps by giving him a free tour of the city or some free drinks. The scammer seems far nicer than most people his victim meets on the street at home, and he puts his victim at ease.

3. When the scammer judges that the victim is sufficiently on the hook, he proposes a deal. He claims to work for a precious stone mine and can get lots of cut stones dirt cheap. He may show an official-looking ID badge, though in many countries these can be bought or faked very cheaply. He claims that if the victim buys them from him at a very good price, the victim can take them back home, and sell them at a huge profit. The scammer will even recommend jewellers back home who will be happy to buy them from the victim.

4. The scammer will say that he appreciates that his victim is not an expert in precious stones, and therefore need to be reassured as to just how much the stones will go for at home. Clippings from newspapers showing gem prices at home appear, and the scammers allow the victim to look them up online. Any doubts which the victim may have are argued away: the scammer is a very good salesman.

5. The scammer offers the victim a full, money-back guarantee, to protect him against any financial loss. Of course, he says, the victim needs to know they are genuine, to ensure that he is not left with worthless paste. The scammer then shows his victim a test which his victim can perform himself, and when he does, it clearly shows the victim that the stones are genuine.

6. The victim buys the gems, and carries them around for the rest of the holiday. An unscrupulous victim smuggles the gems through customs on arrival at his home airport without bothering to pay any duty.

7. The victim then tries to sell them to the jeweller which the scammer recommended, or other jewellers he knows. The jewellers all throw the gems back in the victim's face. They are worthless paste.

The scammer has abused the victim's trust. He has somehow managed to manipulate the test which he insisted the victim conduct on the gems, or else has managed to substitute glass or paste for genuine stones while the victim was not looking. The stones are worthless – cubic zirconium rather than diamonds or coloured glass rather than rubies or emeralds. The victim has lost all his money and has no way of getting back at the scammers. The guarantee they gave the victim is completely worthless. If the victim did not pay duty on the imports, he cannot even complain to the police, otherwise he could find himself being interviewed about smuggling. He has no choice but to write off the money to "experience" and get on with his life.

I have never experienced this particular scam myself, but I know people who have, and travel websites are full of similar stories. It is certainly popular with scammers, particularly in India and in Thailand, where the Tourism Authority receives more than a thousand complaints from victims each year. It relies on most people not being experts on gems or precious metals. Its victims therefore cannot tell what they are buying. Telling genuine gems from fakes is difficult enough for professionals, whom they sometimes fool. For tourists it is almost impossible.

There are a number of ways to avoid this scam:

- If something seems too good to be true, it almost certainly is. Remembering this saying is an incredibly effective way to avoid lots of scams, from e-mail frauds to Madoff-type swindles, and it should perhaps be taught in schools worldwide! To make the same point from the other side of the transaction, scammers say that they can only scam greedy people. If a scammer offers somebody a quick way to make a fortune, the obvious question is why is he not doing it himself? Why is he not a millionaire? Or why is he telling a stranger about the deal, rather than involving one of his close friends or relatives? There are no guaranteed short-cuts to making a fortune, or if there are, they are not likely to be offered to a traveller by a random stranger met in a street or a bar.

- Buying gems to resell them at home is a mug's game. If it is profitable for an individual tourist to make this trade, it is going to be profitable for big companies to do it, so why aren't they? Apart from being illegal unless the tourist pays the crippling duty that his country levies to discourage exactly this practice, the tourist will most likely be landed with fake goods. It is far safer for tourists to buy gems abroad for their beauty or the intrinsic pleasure which they give their buyer. At least that will make sure the tourist gets his money's worth.

- It is better to buy jewellery from reputable-looking stores with well-known brand names, rather than from a person you have just met on the street. The prices may be much higher, and it is unlikely that the tourist will make a fortune by reselling the gems bought at local jewellery stores when he gets home. It may still be possible, or even likely, that a tourist will be swindled at a reputable-looking store, but at least the stones are more likely to be genuine than they are if bought off a person you have just met.

None of these tips, however, guarantee against being sold fake jewellery. The fraudsters who con people in this way are good at what they do, and this scam has been around for a long time. That it is so long-lasting and popular with scammers, despite requiring at least some investment and organisation, shows both that people keep falling for it and that the scammers think that they are fairly unlikely to be caught.

Malaysians caught by gem scam in Thailand

Several Malaysians complain each year about gem scams in Thailand. In 2009, a Malaysian man and his family were taken to a Thai gem shop where the manager claimed that it was the last day of a sale. The manager said that normally the shop would not sell to tourists as it was a wholesale business. The business had an "ISO 9001" banner outside, which helped convince the victims to buy gems. They bought two pendants, a ring and a pair of ear-rings for 130,000 Baht ($4,000/£3,200). When they returned to Malaysia and had the gems inspected, they found out that the gems were fakes. They had been treated with beryllium to change their colour, and were practically worthless.

34. Traditional medicine scams

Likely damage: 2/5

Frequency: 2/5

Countries reported: China, South-East Asia, India, Africa.

Summary: Tourists sold sugary pills instead of traditional medicines.

Many countries have traditions of medical care which differ widely from Western practices. According to the World Health Organisation (WHO), such medicine can sometimes be effective. The WHO notes that "new antimalarial drugs were developed from the discovery and isolation of artemisinin from *Artemisia annua* L., a plant used in China for almost 2000 years". It also says that, in some African and Asian countries, 80 per cent of the population depends on traditional medicine for their primary health care. It defines traditional medicine as "the sum total of knowledge, skills and practices based on the theories, beliefs and experiences indigenous to different cultures that are used to maintain health, as well as to prevent, diagnose, improve or treat physical and mental illnesses". Traditional medicine is also sometimes known as alternative, or complementary, medicine.

The line dividing "traditional" doctors from out-and-out fraudsters is somewhat blurred, however. Not surprisingly, traditional medicines, which are sold mostly in poorer countries, have not undergone the detailed, lengthy and extremely expensive tests which drugs must pass before they may be sold legally in Europe and America. There is, however, evidence that some therapies (such as acupuncture and massage) can be effective for specific conditions. This book takes no view on whether or not these treatments are effective, though it is worth bearing in mind that some traditional medicines use parts of endangered animals, such as rhino horns and tiger skins.

Travellers are often duped into paying too much for medicines which are not the traditional cures they claim to be. When travelling through countries known for traditional medicine, many travellers use the services of clinics which offer this kind of treatment. Not all clinics are what they seem to be, however, and many are businesses which scam money from tourists. The swindlers generally work in the following way:

1. A tour party, fresh from seeing an attraction, will make an unscheduled stop at a traditional medicine clinic.

2. The tourists will be assigned appointments with "doctors" who will ask them if they have any health problems, and diagnose treatments. Most people suffer from some mild health problems, such as aches in their joints or occasional migraines, and herbs or other medicines will be offered to cure them. Even if they do not suffer from them at home, jetlag, pollution and unfamiliar food can bring them out while they travel.

3. If a tourist claims to be in perfect health, the scammers will try and sell him "traditional" treatments for the sort of ailment that almost everybody endures from time to time, such as hangovers or colds.

There is no guarantee that any cures bought from clinics to which tourists are directed by their guides are genuine. It is highly likely that they are selling their victims expensive placebos. Anybody can make a pleasant-smelling blend of herbs and call it "traditional medicine". Even if the clinics are selling their customers the real thing, they will almost certainly be overpriced. There is no regulation on these "clinics" in most countries, and they can charge what they want for their "treatments".

This scam has been reported from many countries, and there are plenty of "alternative medicine" clinics in the developed world too, though these tend to be targeted more at locals rather than at tourists. The scammers are less likely to present themselves as doctors in "clinics" in Africa, and more likely to claim to be shamans or witch doctors. Finding "genuine" traditional medicine is difficult for a foreigner, particularly if he does not speak the language, and does not have a trustworthy local friend. To find "genuine" traditional medicine:

- It may be best to avoid clinics or doctors in areas which see many tourists.

- Researching a clinic or doctor online may also help avoid the better known scammers, though it is much less likely to work with new or obscure clinics.

Travellers should also check that their travel insurance will cover them should they become ill after consuming alternative medicines, since many policies will not.

Alternative medicine scam in Beijing

In 2011, Beijing's tourism department ordered a six-month overhaul of the one-day tour business after it was revealed some retail stores were tricking foreign tourists into buying unnecessary and overpriced traditional Chinese medicine (TCM). The city authorities raided the Nancheng Tianhui medicine store, after a report by Xinhua News Agency on June 8 revealed the franchised outlet of Tongrentang Co Ltd, the largest TCM producer in China, diagnosed foreign tourists brought in by tour guides and charged them exorbitant prices for medicine.

35. Art school scam

Likely damage: 2/5

Frequency: 1/5

Countries reported: China.

Summary: In China, fake art schools sell bad "art" at high prices.

I have always associated this scam with the heavily touristy areas of China, where I have encountered it several times. I have experienced it, and heard of it happening to others, in Beijing and Xi'an, China's ancient capital, near where the famous terracotta warriors are to be found (see example below). Generally speaking, it is simply a high-pressure sales pitch, of the type familiar to potential timeshare or life insurance customers worldwide. Compared with some of the more serious scams in this book, the cost to the victim is generally trivial, but it can still be annoying to be taken for a fool. It is relatively harmless provided that its victims understand what is happening, and refuse to be pressured by the salespeople, but nonetheless travellers constantly fall victim to it, and buy goods which cost them more than they should.

The scam is relatively simple:

1. Young, attractive "art students" who are, in fact, touts, approach tourists and lure them back to their "art school".

2. At the "art school", tourists are pressured to buy art for far more than it is worth.

The scammers will probably not take any more money from its victims than they agree to pay. It is always possible, of course, that the scammers will charge their victims' credit cards twice or sell the numbers to criminals if they pay using plastic, though I have found no reports of this happening. China, the home of this scam, is a country where the criminal law is enforced ruthlessly, and crimes against foreigners are punished particularly harshly. I have, however, heard that it is possible to bargain with the "students" to buy art at a much cheaper price than their initial offer, particularly if done out of earshot of the other customers. It may therefore even be possible to benefit from two hours with a fake art student if you find a painting or a sculpture which you like and if you have the bargaining skills and patience to agree on a sensible price for it. During my own experience of this scam in China, I never felt physically threatened or intimidated, and I was never tricked into buying something which was something else from what I subsequently received.

The dishonest elements of the scam are that:

- The salespeople misrepresent themselves as art students.

- They claim that the work is their own.

- They try and make their victims buy art using "guilt-trips".

- The prices which they charge are extremely high.

- They waste their victims' time.

Assuming you do not wish to pay over the odds for bad artwork, and would rather not be subjected to a high-pressure sales pitch for hours, avoiding this scam is fairly simple once you know what is going on. Simply refuse to go with the touts, no matter how friendly and charming they are, and you will not be scammed. Once they work out that they will not benefit financially from talking to you, they will try and find other victims.

A more difficult question is how to get out of the "art school" without buying something. As so often when dealing with salespeople who are too persistent, everybody has techniques which work for them.

1. Some people simply walk out, ignoring any complaints, but most people feel slightly uncomfortable doing that.

2. Others invent an urgent flight or train journey.

3. Others still say that they have little money with them, and no credit cards.

4. Some simply say, politely and firmly, that they have no interest in the art on sale and will leave now.

Of course, in each case the salesperson is likely to have dealt with your response many times before, and may have a quick reply ready.

My experience of fake art schools in China

The first time I encountered fake art schools, though I did not buy anything, was in Tiananmen Square in Beijing. I was standing at the northern end of Tiananmen Square, near the massive painting of the dictator Mao Zedong whose desecration gave the Chinese government the excuse to murder thousands of student protesters in 1989. As so often in Beijing, the air was so polluted that I was anxious to get moving fairly quickly, despite the historic view. I was just about to take yet another photo of the square when an attractive woman in her early twenties approached me. "Hello", she said – the constant Chinese greeting to all foreigners. "Ni hao", I replied. She said she was a student and asked if she could practice her English on me. After a few words of chit-chat, she got down to her sales pitch. "I am a student in an art school near here. We have many beautiful paintings. Come check it out". As I wanted to get away from the traffic pollution which I could feel accumulating in my throat, I agreed.

We walked to a large, high-ceilinged, well-lit room near the square. There was a big rectangular table in the middle, covered with paintings. The sides of the room were made up of kitchen-style units up to waist height, and the tops were covered with sculptures. There were a few other foreign tourists there, mostly male. They were each talking to a suspiciously good-looking young Chinese woman who was showing them around the room, pointing out art work, and obviously subjecting them to the kind of high pressure sales pitch familiar to anyone who has visited a Moroccan carpet shop or tried to buy a tour of the Pyramids. From their body language, most of the tourists seemed anxious to leave without causing offence, but most of them would probably be talked into buying something. My guide started her sales pitch. The prices of the works of art she showed me were very high, and the quality was pretty low, but she was very persistent and convincing. In the end, however, I was one of those who left without anything, not because I am particularly resistant to sales pitches. I had little cash on me, and had left my credit cards at the hotel where I was staying, so in the end, my "student" obviously decided that her time was better spent trying to find richer travellers.

Chapter 6: Eating, drinking and gambling scams

Drinking in bars is a big part of many people's vacations. Undoubtedly, most people who go to bars have a good time, but many are scammed there. Common sense is often the first casualty of any drinking bout, and scammers love approaching their victims when their inhibitions are down. Scammers can work in bars, or they can be customers of the bar. Bars can charge tourists outrageous amounts of money for drinks.

Casinos and their employees can also sometimes scam their customers. Gamblers are more likely to be scammed, however, by other players. Gambling and betting with strangers outside casinos is not generally recommended. Such games are often rigged, and the victim can lose lots of money in this way.

Finally, restaurants and cafes occasionally scam their customers, though unless they intentionally poison them (see scam #37), the scams are less damaging to travellers than those in bars.

---

36. Clip joints

Likely damage: 4/5

Frequency: 3/5

Countries reported: Any tourist centre with bars.

Summary: Bars lure tourists in and then charge them absurd prices for drinks. They intimidate victims into paying up.

The clip joint scam must have been invented by cavemen. It seems so old and clichéd, but again, it nets victims each year. It is closely related to the no menu scam (see scam #41). It is so well known that it has its own Wikipedia page, and has featured in articles in newspapers such as The New York Times, The Economist and the London Evening Standard. The Wikipedia page, however, focuses on the scam in London and New York, while this swindle has been reported in just about every large tourist city with lots of bars.

As with so many problems from which young men suffer, it starts with a drinking bout and ends with serious trouble. Though it has a thousand variations around the world, it usually runs something like this:

1. The victims, usually a couple of young men, are out exploring the nightlife of a foreign town. They drink enough to be tipsy, but not enough to make them falling-down-drunk. The bar is spinning, but they are not yet flat on their backs.

2. A couple of attractive young women approach them. They may say they want to practice their English (or French, or German).

3. The two couples slip into conversation remarkably easily, and they get on very well with each other. Whatever drunken stupidities the victims come out with, the women take well and manage to laugh. Even some drunken fondling meets with little resistance. The women seem to be enjoying the evening very much.

4. Eventually, one of the women proposes moving to another bar, which is likely to be better in some way: much livelier, or quieter or less smoky.

5. The victims quickly agree, and they finish their drinks. The four walk to a new bar together. This bar, however, is very different from the other. It is down a side street, and almost deserted.

6. The four are allowed in immediately by the bouncer at the door. He does not ask for a cover charge, and the four sit down at a table.

7. The women order champagne and the evening progresses. The men do not think to ask for a menu, and do not ask how much the drinks are.

8. Eventually, the two women go to the bathroom together. They do not come back.

9. The men are then presented with the bill. It comes to several hundred, or even a thousand, dollars. The victims are flabbergasted, and tell the waiter and his extremely tough-looking assistants that they want the women to help to pay. The waiter says that the women have gone home, and demands payment of the bill. If the men refuse, they are physically threatened. If they try to call the police, they are beaten up. If they have credit cards on them, the cards are taken and debited. Any cash they have on them is also stolen. They are then thrown out of the bar, undoubtedly sadder, but hopefully wiser.

The two attractive women who approached the drunks were hustlers employed by the owners of the bar to lure drunken foreign men. This scam relies on the victims being too drunk or too flattered by the attention of beautiful women to ask the price of the services they are getting, before they order them. It also relies on the victims being too ashamed to complain, or else simply wanting to forget the unpleasant evening.

In many cities, these bars operate in a legal grey area, and they can be, and sometimes are, closed down if enough people complain. In other cities, the police are bribed by the bar owners to turn a blind eye in case the victims complain of the extortion to which they are subjected, or refuse to pay. These bars seem to have the vitality of weeds, springing up as often as they are shut down. It only needs a few naive travellers to fall for this swindle for the bar to pay for itself each week.

This scam has many variations:

- Sometimes, it is a man or men who approach the travellers, and lure them to the bar (see example below).

- In America, scammers take advantage of the common practice for bars there to require that customers buy a minimum number of drinks. The minimum is not advertised beforehand, and the drinks in question are priced at several hundred dollars each.

- In London's clip joints, most of which are in the nightlife district of Soho, the bar where the scam takes place is often an explicit sex club.

- Budapest's Vaci Street is the European centre of the scam, which is known in Hungarian as the *konzum lany* (or "consumption girl").

In every such scam, however, the common elements are extortion and intimidation. Victims must feel that they have no choice but to pay outrageous sums to the scammers. Knowing about this scam, and knowing people who have fallen for it, automatically puts people on their guard. There are a number of other tips which should reduce the risk of falling victim to this scam:

- As so often in this book, if something seems too good to be true, it probably is, and being approached by suspiciously friendly men who speak excellent English or by beautiful women who are unusually easy to please should ring lots of alarm bells. The scammers will deliberately pick naive-looking and tipsy men whose alarm bells may not ring when they should.

- Deserted bars without obvious exits, in empty, shady-looking streets are best avoided. Bars that are fairly busy, populated by locals and foreigners alike, evidently having a good time, are much less likely to scam tourists in this way. Dark, empty cellar bars may have an atmosphere that appeals to some people, but they do make it easy for a corrupt management to practice extortion.

- By far the best way to avoid this scam, however, is to demand to know exactly how much drinks will cost. Charging a different sum from that quoted when purchase is agreed is illegal in most countries around the world, and only the worst clip joints will do that. This applies especially in dark, gloomy, empty bars more than in popular bars which are relatively open to a busy street.

- It is also important to demand to know other charges before entering a bar. Bars often rip travellers off with cover charges, hostess charges, charges for VIP access and the costs of drinks themselves.

A clip joint in Las Vegas busted in 2012

Las Vegas Police busted a clip joint called The Red Devil which had operated as follows. Taxi drivers took the (usually drunk) victim to the business. Once a customer paid a $250 "membership fee," the club gave the taxi driver a $200 kickback. The fee got the customer into a room with a scantily-clad attendant who continued to up-sell services with vague language. The customer would be told ambiguous things like, "In the VIP [private rooms], I can touch more places, particularly the 'lower extremities.'"

Before the customer would be led to the back, they would have to sign a form which said no sexual activity will be available. The attendant would assure the victim that the language was a formality. However, the victim's time in the rooms would usually last five minutes and no… ahem… services would be carried out.

Police had been called to the club several times in a few months. One of those calls followed the stabbing of a tourist from the United Kingdom by an employee. Police believe that suspect fled immediately after the stabbing. Police also said most customers did not call police because they did not want to be revealed as soliciting prostitution. In addition, police believed that victims thought that, since they had signed an agreement, the contract would be used against them because no illegal activity was committed.

Six others believed to be employees at the club were arrested following the stabbing incident.

A friend foils a clip joint in Istanbul

In Istanbul in 1997, my travelling companion accidentally hit upon an interesting way of avoiding paying hundreds of dollars when targeted by this scam, but it could be dangerous, and so is definitely not recommended. He had *so little* money on him that the bouncer found it all rather funny and let him go. He had been lured into a bar by a (male) scammer, who had promised him that he would have drinks provided for free. When the bill of several hundred dollars for a couple of bottles of fake champagne was presented to him by a bouncer, however, he could not pay because he only had seven dollars (a million lire in the Turkish money of the time) on him and no credit cards. The thug burst out laughing: "this does not even buy one cigarette at this club", he said. He let my friend go uninjured. When he came back to the hotel room we were sharing, my friend told me that he had been extremely lucky that they did not beat him up.

37. Poisoning insurance scam

Likely damage: 5/5

Frequency: 1/5

Countries reported: India.

Summary: Corrupt restauranteurs poison travellers' food and call a doctor of their choice. They then split the travel insurance money with the hospital.

Virtually all cases of food poisoning in travellers are accidental – the result of unhygienic preparation of food by chefs, or of travellers' unfamiliarity with local bugs. "Delhi belly" in India, "Bali Belly" in Indonesia, "Pharaoh's Revenge" in Egypt and

"Montezuma's Revenge" in Mexico are all different names for this form of sickness.

Almost everybody who ever travels in a developing country for any length of time will get slightly sick in this way, often several times. In these cases, doctors commonly recommend rest and rehydration, with a visit to a surgery for more serious food poisoning.

This scam is the stuff of urban nightmares, but it does seem to be *rare*, and confined to a few places around the world, in particular some towns in India. Following a crackdown by police in Agra, it seems to be less common now than it was ten years ago. It runs as follows:

1. The scammers are members of the staff of a restaurant. They put poison in a dish which they prepare, using a drug which will put the victim in hospital, but not kill.

2. Having poisoned the customer, the scammers then rush the victim to hospital as quickly as possible, where the victim sees a doctor who is in on the plot, and therefore knows exactly what is wrong with the victim and therefore knows how to heal him or her.

3. The victim's travel insurance pays the doctor for his work.

4. The profit from this scam comes from the large fees which the hospital and its doctors can charge the victim's insurance company. The scammers in the staff of the restaurant split the proceeds with the corrupt doctor.

The poisoners could go too far and could kill a victim rather than simply send him or her to hospital (see the example below). Miscalculating a dosage or feeding somebody something to which they are allergic are fairly common in poisoning cases, and sometimes have fatal results. This scam is (potentially) one of the most dangerous there is, though the idea is not to kill the tourist but to make profit from the insurance company.

Detecting the scam is difficult for the same reason that it is so effective in the first place. People trust their doctors, especially when they have just saved them remarkably rapidly from an unpleasant condition. It would never occur to most people that the person who has just treated them might have helped cause the problem.

If the victim does not have travel insurance, he or she is not only poisoned, but can be stuck with a bill running into thousands of dollars for the privilege. The victim can refuse to pay, but most likely will be forced to pay at least some of the money demanded, unless he has no money at all.

Virtually everybody who travels at all will eat in a restaurant at some point, and many tourists eat most of their meals out. Because this scam is so sneaky, it is difficult to take steps to avoid it until it is too late. Tourist authorities in Agra and Varanassi urge visitors to stick to government-approved hotels, guides and restaurants, but this is perhaps going too far. While there may be a tiny chance of being poisoned in some cities, avoiding local restaurants simply because of this or similar scams really is throwing the baby out with the bathwater. But knowing that this scam happens, however rare it may be, could at least enable a traveller to point the police in the right direction if one is unlucky enough to be victimised in this way.

Two Irish tourists killed by poisoning in Varanassi, India

Two Irish tourists, Eoin McGowan and Aidan Geraghty, were poisoned in 1998 in Varanasi, India. The poisoners evidently overdosed the dish which they fed the victims with poison. The two tourists collapsed and died.

Korean tourist poisoned in Agra, India

In November 1998, a Korean tourist in Agra fainted after being fed lassi and an omelette outside her hotel. After a police investigation, it was determined that the hotel had conspired to defraud the victim's insurance company.

38. Spiked drinks in bars

Likely damage: 4/5

Frequency: 2/5

Countries reported: Any tourist centre with bars.

Summary: A traveller in a bar is offered a drugged drink. The traveller is robbed and may be sexually assaulted.

This scam is international and has been around for centuries. It has been reported across many countries, and both locals and tourists are victims. Though it has many variations, the course of events is similar in all of them:

1. The victim is in a bar where one or more scammers approach him and they get talking.

2. The scammer offers to buy drinks.

3. The victim accepts.

4. While the victim is not looking, the scammer drops some drugs into the drink.

5. The victim loses consciousness and wakes up hours later, having been robbed or sexually assaulted, or both.

The victims are not necessarily tourists: this scam is perpetrated far more often on locals than on travellers. Tourists are often targeted in tourist centres, however, especially in Thailand, India and Latin America. 44 foreign tourists reported being targeted in this way in Hong Kong between 2004 and 2007, though many cases probably go unreported, particularly if the victims were uninsured and therefore did not need a police report to make a claim.

The United States Drug Enforcement Administration calls the chemicals used in this scam "predatory drugs". They are odourless and tasteless. The effect of the drugging on the traveller depends on the drug used, but some of them also wipe the victim's memory, so that he or she cannot tell the police what happened and cannot describe the robber. There have been several reported cases of travellers being killed through probably unintentional overdoses of sedatives in spiked drinks (see examples below). Many powerful sedatives, such as Rohypnol, have been used to drug tourists in bars. The problem was so serious in the late 1990's that the manufacturers of Rohypnol started adding a blue dye to the drug to make it visible in drinks. Unfortunately, bootleg versions, which do not contain the colouring, are relatively freely available.

In the northern part of South America, a drug commonly used is burundanga. It can also be used in a tourist's food or cigarettes, though rumours that people can be drugged through touching business cards or flyers coated with the drug are unfounded. It is a derivative of the plant which was used by the Chibcha people to sedate a dead chief's widow and slaves before they were buried alive with him. In Bogota, Colombia, it accounts for around half of all poisonings. People who ingest significant quantities often experience hallucinations, disorientation and a loss of vision.

There are ways to minimise the likelihood of falling victim to this scam, if you are in a city or country which is notorious for it:

- It is advisable to buy bottled drinks at bars, rather than drinks served in glasses. Because bottles have narrow necks, it is more difficult to drop drugs into them unobserved.

- It is also better to be slightly suspicious of people who approach you in a bar while you are travelling, rather than the other way around, especially if they seem effusively friendly and speak English much better than most people you have met (assuming that you are in a non-English-speaking country).

- Another worrying sign is if people insist on buying you drinks, and manoeuvre so that the glasses or bottles are out of your sight, even if only for a few seconds.

- Be careful leaving drinks unattended; if you go to the toilet – take your beer with you.

- Leaving cash and valuables in your hotel is also a good way to reduce the likelihood of being targeted (and the loss you suffer if you are targeted).

- Going out with someone you trust should also reduce the chance that you will be a victim, as thieves may be more likely to approach single travellers.

British tourist drugged and robbed in Manila

You do not have to be on public transport to be drugged and robbed. In 2017, I was in Manila and got talking to the owner of my guesthouse. He told me that an English guest of his had been befriended by a Filipino couple the month before. They had taken him back to their apartment and fed and watered him. He had been drugged and fell asleep. After he woke up and got back to the hotel, he discovered from his bank that approximately £15,000/$20,000 had been spent on his credit card. Fortunately, the bank did not make him pay that large amount.

British expat drugged, robbed and killed in Russia

In December 2016, a 22-year-old British expat, living in Russia, went missing. According to his mother, he, his brother, and a female friend were offered a lift by some people who said they would take them to a party. On the way, they were offered a beer which was spiked. They were then kicked out of the car. The man became separated from his brother and the female friend, and died of hypothermia in the freezing Russian winter conditions.

Bali expat drugged and seriously affected

In July 2016, a Western woman who lives in Bali claimed that she was drugged with 'multiple doses' of Rohypnol while drinking at a bar in north Kuta. Upon leaving the bar, she fell to the ground, splitting her face open before projectile vomiting and nearly going into organ failure. She documented her ordeal on Facebook.

The Australian Government Department of Foreign Affairs and Trade warns travellers to be "aware of the specific risks from … drink-spiking and consumption of alcohol adulterated with harmful substances such as methanol".

British tourist couple drugged and sexually assaulted in Thailand

In 2009, a British couple were ending their year off in Ko Chang, Thailand. They had a pleasant drink in a bar with some other tourists. At some point, their drinks were spiked, apparently by the other tourists, who carried them back to their bungalow to rape and sexually assault the pair.

Three tourists killed by spiked drinks

In 2001, a young Irish tourist was found dead in a park in Prague, after consuming a spiked drink in a city centre bar. A toxicology examination showed that he had drunk the sedatives Rohypnol and Diazepam. A friend of his was found unconscious near his body. Police believed his friend had also been drugged. Three women were subsequently arrested.

Spiked cappuccinos

In 2009, an American tourist and his wife were visiting Rome after cruising in the Mediterranean. They met a man in a café and accepted cappuccinos which he bought for them. The drinks contained a cocktail of drugs, including sleeping pills. When they were intoxicated, the scammer robbed them. The male American tourist then apparently wandered, dazed, onto railway tracks and was killed by an oncoming train. His wife was briefly hospitalised.

39. Casino scams

Likely damage: 3/5

Frequency: 2/5

Countries reported: Wherever people gamble.

Summary: How tourists are scammed by casinos and fellow gamblers.

Millions of travellers visit the tourist cities of Las Vegas, Atlantic City, Monte Carlo and Macau each year, mainly to gamble at the casinos there. Many more visit casinos in other, less well known, gambling spots. Every year, thousands of gamblers try to cheat the casinos using an unbelievable variety of scams. This section, however, is about the ways in which gamblers are scammed, either by the casino and its employees, or, more often, by fellow gamblers.

Each year, many tourists are scammed by corrupt casino employees. It is impossible in this space to mention more than a few of the ways in which dealers can scam players. Dealers often make both actual and fraudulent mistakes when they pay out, meaning that either they, or the casino, keep a part of the victim's winnings. In one scam:

1. The victim is playing a game with a croupier or dealer, such as blackjack or roulette.

2. The victim's number comes up on a roulette wheel, entitling him to 36 times his original stake.

3. The croupier may pay him only 35 times the original stake, and since most of us are not quick enough at multiplying large numbers in our heads to notice the difference, the victim may not notice the "mistake".

The scam can only succeed if the victim does not know how much he stands to win: working this out beforehand is the best defence against being scammed in this way.

Apparently legitimate casinos sometimes attempt to rip gamblers off by refusing to pay jackpots which players have legitimately won, if they can claim that the machines are defective. Strangely, however, they never pay back gamblers who have *lost* money to defective machines. It is often not clear whether casinos are acting unlawfully when they refuse to pay out. In this case, casinos often pay out eventually if the gambler makes enough noise or threatens to take them to court (see examples below).

Sometimes, in games such as blackjack, the dealer may be cooperating with one of the players, dealing him better cards. In helping that player to win, he may try to make the other players lose, to preserve the profits on that table and so conceal his fraud from the casino. It is easiest for a corrupt dealer to do this by rigging the shuffle. To avoid being scammed in this way, therefore, it is better to play blackjack using automatic shufflers.

Another casino scam is a "distraction" swindle, involving a two-person team:

1. The victim is at a gambling table, with a large stack of chips in front of him. He may be tipsy or drunk, and therefore not at his most observant.

2. One of the scammers is an attractive and unusually friendly woman who ingratiates herself with the victim and wishes him good luck.

3. While the victim's attention is distracted, her partner steals from the victim's piles of chips. Since the piles of chips are so large, it is unlikely that the victim will notice.

These thieves tend to keep clear of big casinos, which are very heavily guarded and have CCTV cameras everywhere, and commit their robberies in smaller casinos or hotels.

Sometimes, other gamblers try to swindle travellers in casinos. The scammers try to rig the games against their victims. As in the distraction scam above, the victim may well not notice, especially if the casino is feeding him free alcoholic drinks to keep him gambling. Poker is a game in which it is possible for two or more colluding players to scam money from the remainder of the table.

Even a simple device like speaking in a language which is not understood by the other players can give two gamblers a significant advantage if they use this private code to exchange information about their cards. Teams of swindlers can also use eye and hand signals and hidden electronic communication. Most casinos allow gamblers to sit where they like so teams of scammers can sit at the same poker game and cheat other players. See the example below for a bizarre story about a rigged poker game in Atlantic City.

Three American casinos refuse to pay when gamblers hit jackpots

In 2006, a California man was playing five cent slots when the machine told him that he had won $723,000. The casino refused to pay, claiming that the machine had malfunctioned and that the maximum prize for that particular machine should have been $2,500.

In 2007, a slot machine in Philadelphia told a man that he had won $102,000. The casino claimed that a mechanical error had meant that the notification had been given even though the symbols had not lined up. It offered the man a couple of free visits to the buffet but refused to pay out. According to the Philadelphia Daily News, the man commented, "I'm thinking to myself, they do have a nice steakhouse there. They didn't even give me that. They're giving me the buffet. That buffet must be one helluva buffet". The man hired an attorney and eventually forced the casino to pay him the money it had told him he had won.

In 1999, a slot machine in an Arizona casino told a gambler that she had won $330,000. The casino refused to pay, saying that the machine had a defective computer chip. She went to the press, and the casino eventually paid her the jackpot in full.

Poker game rigged in Atlantic City, New Jersey

Poker is one of the most popular card games in the United States, and is becoming increasingly widespread worldwide. In 2007, four men were arrested in Atlantic City and charged with attempted theft. They had set up electronic surveillance in two rooms at the Borgata Hotel and Spa to rig the game. They then invited a man to play high-stakes Chinese poker with them.

The scammers intended to use the equipment to monitor the poker from the second room. The victim was to play an opponent who was part of the alleged scheme. The scammers allegedly planned to use marked playing cards for the Chinese poker so they could identify the victim's cards and transmit instructions to the opposing player, who would be wearing a hidden earpiece. Police raided the rooms before their victim arrived.

Three of the four men were later convicted and given suspended sentences. The charges against the other man were dropped.

40. Rigged betting game scams

Likely damage: 2/5

Frequency: 3/5

Countries reported: Global.

Summary: Light relief: how tourists are encouraged to make bets they cannot win.

Scammers love approaching tourists in bars. Their victims are generally friendlier and more communicative. They often have large amounts of cash on them, and they are often tipsy, lowering their resistance. There are any number of ways in which people can be separated from their cash using so-called "sucker bets", and the number of such bets is always growing. There are some old favourites, however, and this section of the book lists a few.

Most are fairly clever, even amusing, if you do not happen to be a victim, and a scammer rarely makes much money from them. All but the dimmest drunks will be suspicious if a stranger in a bar offers to bet thousands of dollars with them on a bet he seems certain to lose. A good example of such a bet runs as follows:

1. The scammer promises the victim that he will only charge him $50/£40 to show how to cut his electricity bill in half.

2. If the victim agrees, the scammer will produce an electricity bill and a rusty pair of scissors, and proceed to cut the bill in two.

3. The scammer will then demand the victim's money, possibly offering him the scissors as a free gift.

Another sucker bet which plays on the victim's misunderstanding of what the scammer said involves coins. Similar games can be played with any country's coinage, though in this example, I have assumed that the scam takes place in America:

1. The scammer will show his victim his closed fist.

2. He offers to bet his victim that he has in his hand two coins whose value adds up to 35 cents, "and one of them ISN'T a quarter [25 cents]".

3. The victim will therefore take the bet, as the only way to make 35 cents using two US coins is with a dime [ten cents] and a quarter.

4. The scammer will open his hand and reveal a dime and a quarter. He had only said that ONE of the coins was not a quarter, rather than that BOTH of the coins were not quarters. He has therefore made 35 cents with two coins "and one of them ISN'T a quarter", though the other IS.

5. He will therefore claim that he has won his bet, and ask his victim to pay up.

Another sucker bet involving a play on words is connected with professional sports:

1. The scammer picks a well-known trophy match, such as the Superbowl Final in America, or the FA Cup Final, the greatest club football match in England. The remainder of this example assumes that the scam takes place in England.

2. He announces that he knows something about the next FA Cup Final. It will be between Brentford and Barnet, two indifferent London teams.

3. As neither team has a hope of reaching the Final, the victim will be tempted to take the bet, if he knows anything about sport.

4. The scammer will claim, however, that the FA Cup Final will indeed be *between* Brentford and Barnet: Wembley Stadium in north-west London, where the Final is traditionally played, is located geographically between Brentford in west London and Barnet in north London.

5. Again, the scammer will claim that he has won the bet, and ask the victim for his money.

In yet another sucker bet, the swindler puts an unopened bottle of beer on the table, and bets his victim that he can drink beer from the bottle without opening it in any way. If the victim accepts, the swindler turns the bottle upside down and pours a few drops of beer from another bottle onto the indentation in the outside of the bottom of the original bottle. He then drinks the beer he has just poured. He has therefore drunk from the original bottle without opening it. This bet works just as well with unopened wine bottles.

Other sucker bets involve games of chance:

1. The scammer approaches a tourist in a bar.

2. He proposes a game of dice, in which he offers the victim odds on rolling a given number. He happens to have a pair of dice in his pocket.

3. If the dice are fair, there is a known probability of a given outcome.

4. The victim bets his money on this assumption.

5. In fact, the scammer's dice are loaded so that he will win rather more often than he should, and, providing the game goes on long enough, he is virtually guaranteed to end up ahead.

Since the scammer loses as well as wins, however, it would take a rigorous mathematical analysis of the game to spot that the dice could be loaded, and even then the analysis could not prove conclusively that the game was rigged. What works with loaded dice also works with marked playing cards.

The key feature of these bets is that the victim has very little, or no, chance of winning, or of coming out ahead, but thinks that he does. The difficulty from the scammer's point of view is not to win the bet, but to persuade the victim to pay up afterwards. If the bet is not obviously rigged in the scammer's favour, he may try to convince the victim that she has simply been unlucky. The victim may then feel that the bet was not rigged, and therefore that she has not been swindled and should pay up. This does not usually work in bets where the victim clearly had no chance of winning, such as the FA Cup or beer bottle tricks above, but it may work better in games where the scammer loses as well as wins, such as the unfair dice game mentioned above. It will also work if the scammer uses marked playing cards, and other rigged gambling devices.

This is one family of scams where the simplest way of avoiding being swindled is the best: do not make drunken bets with strangers in bars, or if you do, expect to lose what you bet. As always with gambling, people who do make such bets should only bet money that they can afford to lose.

41. "No menu" scam

Likely damage: 2/5

Frequency: 3/5

Countries reported: Global, particularly common in poor countries which see a lot of tourists.

Summary: A tourist buys drinks at a café without asking the price, which turns out to be much higher than it should be.

This family of scams is similar to the clip joint scam (see scam #45 above), which targets drunken male travellers in bars. These swindles can target people who would not normally go to bars and do not attempt to lure patrons in with attractive women or misleading advertising, and so they deserve their own section in this book. Though there are many variants, most run as follows:

1. The victim orders drinks in a cafe, or food in a restaurant.

2. The menu does not have prices, and the victim does not think to ask how much the drink or food costs.

3. When the bill comes, it is far higher than it should be.

As so often, travellers are relatively susceptible to these scams because they are not familiar with local price levels and customers. They are less likely to complain than locals and in many countries they are richer than most locals, and hence easier to fleece. Perhaps above all, they are out for a good time and are not looking to spoil their holiday with arguments about a few dollars.

From the two examples below, these scams may appear to be an Eastern European speciality, but, unfortunately, they are more widespread than that. In Morocco, tourists sometimes eat lunch at hole-in-the-wall sandwich bars. Customers usually pay after they have eaten, and prices can be much higher if the customer is a tourist. I have heard of similar scams in Thailand, Vietnam and in some South America countries. I doubt that they are limited to these places: wealthy, foreign tourists frequent cafés all over the world. The amount of money lost by the victim who has been swindled in this way is usually small, but the feeling of anger is often much greater than the small sum seems to warrant.

Related to the "no menu" scam is the "new price" scam:

1. The victim finds something he wants to buy while shopping, or he may be in a café and about to pay the bill.

2. He is presented with a bill which is much higher than its price tag, or than the menu, led him to believe.

3. He complains to the waiter or shop assistant, and even asks to see their manager.

4. The scammer tells the victim that the price he saw was the "old price" – prices have just gone up since the list was printed. This may be the case, but it is more likely that the waiter thinks the victims will simply pay up and leave, rather than bother to argue over the difference.

If the victim refuses to pay the "new price", the scammer can sell the victim what he wants to buy at the original price and the business will have lost nothing.

A related scam occurs in restaurants:

1. Food, in particular, meat or fish, will be priced on the menu by weight.

2. The restaurant staff, however, will provide their customer with much less meat or fish than they charge her for, or they will charge her by weight for meat or fish which is mostly bone.

3. As the customer does not have scales with her, she will not be able to work out the price she should be paying, and will most likely pay the restaurant what it asks.

Many seafood restaurants do not include prices for dishes involving fresh fish. They often list the price for these meals as "market price". This is not usually a scam, since the market price of fresh fish can vary dramatically day by day. However, there is no excuse for changing prices of items like coffee dramatically, just because the café happens to be serving tourists rather than locals. I learned in Bosnia to be suspicious of a café or a restaurant which does not produce a menu (see the example below), and especially of one which does not show a price list when asked. Since then, I have never assumed that I know what a price is, but have tried to remember to ask before I order. However, what I have learned from my friend's experience in Budapest (another example below), is that even when I think I know the price, I can still be swindled. Other than refusing to pay, or paying and then reporting the restaurant to the tourist police, if there are any, there does not seem much that a tourist can do to frustrate a waiter who decides to double the price of a drink on a whim, and without telling him.

My experience of a "no menu" scam in Bosnia

In 2009, I was in Mostar, Bosnia, a delightful town centred on a famous bridge ("Most" in Bosnian) over the River Neretva. The Bosnian economy was at a standstill. Tourism was therefore a huge industry, and, as always, some businesses were dishonest. I was there in June, and after two hours of walking around the Old Town with three friends in the baking sunshine, I was ready for some refreshment. We found a café with shaded benches and cushions on the ground on which to recline and sprawled on the floor. The four of us had five coffees, a cup of tea and a couple of pastries between us.

Prices in Bosnia were low compared to Western Europe, so we were surprised when the bill came to almost twenty euros (then $28/£18). In most other cafes in Mostar, it would have come to no more than eight or ten euros. When we asked for the menu to check the prices, the waiter pretended he did not have one available. As the additional amount was relatively small, we paid and left, but decided never to go to that café again. When I got back to my hotel, I heard by chance from the manager that that particular café was notorious for charging foreigners extra if they did not ask for a menu. In that case, the café would automatically double its prices, or increase them even further if the foreigners looked like they could afford it.

"No menu" scam in Hungary

A friend experienced a variation of this scam at a café in central Budapest. He ordered a beer, and had the foresight to ask how much it would cost. He was told that it would be 600 Hungarian Forints – about $2/£1.50 at the time. In the course of a pleasant afternoon's drinking, he ordered several beers. Eventually, he came to ask for the bill. He was unpleasantly surprised when it he saw that the waiter had charged the first beer at 600 Forints, as they had said, but had charged subsequent beers at 1,000 Forints ($4/£2.50 at the time). He refused to pay, and disputed the charges with the waiter. The waiter insisted that he pay. My friend called the manager, who also insisted that he pay, and called security when he refused. The big security guard intimidated my friend, who eventually decided that he did not need the hassle and paid up. Though the unjustified charges for the beer did not cost my friend more than $16/£10, the experience soured his opinion of Budapest, which he had been enjoying, and he left earlier than he had expected.

42. Refilled bottled water scam

Likely damage: 4/5

Frequency: 2/5

Countries reported: Countries without clean tap water, in particular India and Nepal.

Summary: Scammers in India in particular get hold of empty bottles, fill them with tap water and market them as bottled water.

In America and Europe, many people contend that buying bottled water, which is often simply bottled tap water, is not necessary and that the whole industry is a scam. In Egypt, India, Nepal and many other poorer countries, however, tap water can be harmful, particularly if a tourist is not used to drinking it there. Standards of water purity are far lower in the developing world than in America or Europe. An impressive number of diseases, including cholera, typhoid fever and dysentery can be caused by drinking infected water. Bottled water literally saves lives every day.

A tourist may drink, and even brush her teeth, using only bottled water, but tap water can still find its way into her system. Ice in drinks is often made using tap water and vegetables in a tourist's salad may be cleaned with it. The traditional solution for problems with the local water is to carry a hip flask with gin or whisky, and mix the spirit with any drinks made with the local water.

Strong alcohol should kill the worst of the germs in the water. It is not always possible to find spirits, however, and even if it is, a traveller may not want to dilute drinking water in this way. Many tourists therefore rely on bottled water, and all too often assume that it is safe.

However, a common scam in developing countries is to tamper with bottled water. The criminals fill an empty water bottle with tap water, and reseal it, passing it off as bottled water. They can then sell it at a much higher price than they could get for a bottle of tap water. They target tourists, who are used to paying high prices for bottled water at home, even when they can get clean and safe tap water for free. Often, bottles of tap water will be sold with straws already inserted. In that case, the bottle has certainly already been opened, and a tourist should be very careful before drinking from it.

Even examining the seal on the neck of the bottle and checking that it has not been broken does not guarantee that the water is safe to drink. Scammers often make a hole in the bottom of an empty water bottle and refill it using tap water. They then plug the hole using plastic and resell it as bottled water. In some countries, including India, water bottles display warnings asking people to crush the bottles thoroughly when they have finished with them, to ensure that scammers do not refill them.

Making sure that bottled water is what it claims to be is therefore difficult. The only way to be sure that the water is reasonably safe is to boil it for ten or twenty minutes and then filter it. There are some tips to reduce the probability of drinking unsafe water, however:

- In a bar or restaurant, ask whether the ice cubes are made using water which has been boiled and then filtered, and whether any drinking glass or cup has been washed with water treated in this way.

- Iodine tablets can be used to purify suspect water.

- In practice, it is rarely possible to be sure that water bought on the street or from food stores has been purified. Large food stores or supermarkets are less likely to scam tourists with fake bottled water than street vendors.

- Bottled water in restaurants should be treated with suspicion, and it is probably safer to order branded soft drinks like Coca Cola, which are much safer, while making sure that the restaurant does not use ice made from tap water.

43. Tea ceremony scam

Likely damage: 2/5

Frequency: 2/5

Countries reported: China, Ethiopia.

Summary: Fake tea ceremonies admit tourists at very high prices.

This scam is similar to the Chinese art school (see scam #44), in that it exploits foreigners' curiosity about Chinese culture to make them pay far over the odds for a tacky parody of the original. Tea ceremonies have been an important part of Chinese culture for centuries, and many tourists consider that attending one is one of the highlights of their holiday in the People's Republic. Traditionally, these rituals are used to show respect to others, as part of a wedding, or to apologise to people for minor insults.

Inevitably, as China has attracted more tourists over the past two decades, tea ceremonies have been organised for foreigners. These more commercial ceremonies are rather like commercial wine tastings. The tourist is allowed to sample small quantities of different types of tea, usually for free, and can then buy more if he or she wants. I have been to one ceremony in Beijing and another in a small town near Wuhan. In neither case was the price unreasonable. The ceremony near Wuhan stands out in my memory because it was before the Chinese tourist industry was as efficient as it is today. The tea was delicious and the person who was pouring it gave us what was doubtless an extremely polished and interesting guide to the place of tea in Chinese philosophy, history and culture. However, neither the Canadian couple I was visiting nor I could understand a word of her long explanation, as it was all in Mandarin. Towards the end, she seemed to realise the absurdity of it, and broke down in giggles while she was talking to us, which detracted from what was clearly meant to be a solemn, almost religious, ritual, especially as the giggles were infectious. It was an amusing way to spend an evening.

As China has opened up to tourists, its scammers have realised that there is some money to be made from swindling foreigners. Holding an overpriced tea ceremony for the benefit of travellers is an extremely common and popular scam in areas of China which are on the tourist trail, in particular Beijing and Shanghai. Tourists make tempting targets because they are far richer than most Chinese, and have no idea what a tea ceremony should cost.

Tea ceremony scammers target foreigners in the following way:

1. Touts hang out in the most heavily touristy areas of Beijing or Shanghai, or near their hotels. They often claim to be interested in improving their English.

2. Scammers also advertise with flyers in English and other western languages. Neither the flyers nor the touts mention a price, though they say that the advertiser accepts credit cards.

3. Travellers are then lured to the advertiser's premises. The ceremony starts, usually with the offer of samples of the various types of tea. An English speaker then feeds the traveller more and more tea, until he has had enough, while explaining to his victim the importance of the drink in Chinese culture.

4. The victim is then offered the opportunity to buy the various blends he has been fed. He will, most likely, be having a good time until he is presented with the bill.

The bill for a legitimate two hour tea ceremony (excluding any tea the tourist wants to buy) may be Y200/$25/£20. I have, however, heard of the bill for some tea ceremonies being ten or 15 times the figure I quoted. The victim will have been charged for all the samples he was given, though he was led to believe that they would be usually free. The charge for the ceremony itself will be extortionate. And then he will be charged top whack for the teas he has bought.

The moral is, of course, familiar to those who have read the "clip joints" scam (see scam #36) and the "no menu" scam (see scam #41). Travellers should always be sure that they know exactly what they are paying for, and how much it will cost, unless they are completely sure that the business they are dealing with is legitimate. Not asking the price before you buy is an invitation to unscrupulous businesses to swindle. Even the most honest will be tempted to raise their prices slightly, if the tourist has not asked the price beforehand.

There are two further tips to avoid becoming a victim of this scam:

- When attending a tea ceremony, you should be very suspicious of businesses or ceremonies to which you are lured by locals who have just befriended you. It is unwise to assume that anything will be free, or that people are doing things for tourists' benefit without expecting to be paid. Even if they do not intend to swindle you, they will very likely expect you to give them far more money than is considered normal.

- Any tourist with no, or very little, money on them, should say so at the start. And, if you do fall for a scam like this, you can at least take comfort in knowing that many experienced travellers have also been tricked in this way.

Similar scams have been reported in other countries around the world. The so-called "siren scam" in Ethiopia is clearly related (see below). Most tourists suffer relatively little damage from these swindles. Some tourists who are presented with bills will pay them without even realising that they have been scammed. Victims are not usually intimidated or physically threatened. The bills are not outrageous enough to hurt any but the poorest travellers seriously. The scammers are often wise to count on the fact that most tourists will not know what an appropriate price would be for witnessing an exotic ritual, and even if the victim refuses to pay, the scammers will have lost little.

"Siren scam" in Ethiopia

In 2008, a friend of mine was travelling through Ethiopia. He was lured to a private house with the promise of being shown Ethiopian cultural activities, such as "traditional" dancing or an Ethiopian wedding. He was given some unconvincing traditional dancing and some overpriced drinks. As Ethiopia is a very cheap country, he was expecting a bill of $10/£8, instead of the $50/£40 which he was asked to pay. He eventually managed to negotiate the bill down to $15/£12.

Chapter 7: Government scams

All too often, governments, like touts and swindlers worldwide, see tourists as easy meat. They like to squeeze as much money as they can out of them, because tourists do not vote in countries which they visit. Given that governments around the world have a huge appetite for other people's money, it is perhaps surprising that they do not tax tourists more than they do. The next few scams show some of the more outrageous ways in which governments make money from tourists.

Government scams are much more difficult to avoid than private sector scams, because they usually have the force of law behind them. The only legal way to avoid hiring a guide to Turkmenistan, for example, is not to visit the country. Some travellers in fact DO refuse to visit countries where the visa regime is particularly onerous, but all too often, this involves missing out on some wonderful parts of the world.

44. Foreigner charges scam

Likely damage: 1/5

Frequency: 2/5

Countries reported: India, Indonesia, Sri Lanka, Guatemala.

Summary: Museums and other attractions charge foreigners many times what the locals pay.

"Foreigner pricing" for museums or sights is fairly widespread in the developing world, and often infuriates its victims. It could be the most brazen, and maddening, official swindle there is. There are few things more guaranteed to make people see red than being discriminated against because of their nationality and there are also few annoyances which rile most people more than being scammed but being powerless to prevent it.

I am not talking here about the common practice of charging tourists more in a market, where bargaining is expected and the victim can go to another stall. I am talking about an official decision that foreigners should pay more than locals for admission to museums and other attractions. This is a scam because there is absolutely no reason why foreigners should pay more to visit the Taj Mahal or the Mayan ruins at Tikal than locals do. It is clearly discrimination, which is illegal in some countries, and highly frowned upon in many others. But governments or tourist agencies think they can make some extra cash from tourists, and so foreigner prices are spreading.

There might be some excuse for this scam – though it would of course still be discrimination – if rich locals had to pay more than poor locals or broke travellers. This is never the case however – foreigners are ripped off because of where they come from, rather than their relative wealth or poverty. A penniless foreign traveller, therefore, pays many times what a local multi-millionaire pays.

As so often with governmental scams, the gains seem much less than the indirect costs to the government's country. Around 200,000 foreigners visit the Taj Mahal in Agra, India's best known tourist attraction, each year. They pay $20 each to visit, while Indians pay a few cents. Raising an extra $4 million from foreigners is spare change even for the Indian Government (though travellers can feel happy that they are contributing a trivial amount towards India's nuclear weapon and space programmes). And, as nobody enjoys feeling ripped off, it annoys many travellers, though all, of course, understand why the Government of India does it.

Many poorer countries refuse to discriminate against travellers in this way, despite needing money as much as those that do. They refuse to rip tourists off, just because they are easy targets. I have never had to pay more to visit tourist attractions just because of my nationality in Malaysia or Bolivia, for instance. This shows that poor countries do not need to swindle foreigners like this. It is a conscious policy choice to gouge money for a poorer country's treasury.

As with most official scams, avoiding being stung in this way is difficult, without breaking the law or swindling the swindlers in some way. Boycotting countries which behave in this way means missing out on some unforgettable experiences in countries which, overall, are extremely cheap to visit. This is one of those scams where travellers just have to "grin and bear it".

The amounts which this scam costs travellers are rarely enough to damage most people's budgets significantly, unless they are visiting a number of these sights. No travellers on medium or high budgets are likely to notice the $20 it costs for foreigners to visit the Taj Mahal, or the $15 extra that it costs them to visit Tikal, and even those on the lowest budgets will not be badly affected because of these extra charges. It is therefore not the most damaging scam covered in this book, though it may well be one of the most irritating.

Foreigner charges at tourist attractions

As this practice is so widespread, it is impossible in this space to list all the tourist attractions which charge foreigners much more than locals. Besides Tikal in Guatemala, I have encountered it:

- In Indonesia in 2014, I was charged $30 to climb a volcano, while Indonesians paid $2. I refused to pay.

- In India, where a visit to the Taj Mahal costs 15 rupees (30 US cents) to Indians, but 960 rupees ($20) to foreigners.

- In Sri Lanka, at the fabulous 5th century cliff palace of Sigiriya, which, when I visited in 2003, cost local Sri Lankans 20 rupees, but foreigners an eye-popping 72 times as much, 1440 rupees.

- In Syria and Jordan, too, foreigners pay far more than locals for visits to many attractions. Admission to the spectacular city of Petra, for example, costs foreigners 33 Jordanian Dinar ($50/£40), but Jordanians pay only 2 Dinar ($3/£2.50).

The practice is certainly most common in developing countries, but it occasionally bites tourists in the western world. England's Windsor Castle, for example, allows residents of the Borough of Windsor and Maidenhead to take tours for free, while charging everybody else a steep £16/$25.

45. Exit tax scams

Likely damage: 2/5

Frequency: 2/5

Countries reported: Central America, Israel, Egypt, Jordan.

Summary: Governments charge tourists for the privilege of being allowed to go home, even overland.

At the end of 2009, I was in Flores, Guatemala, sitting in one of the lakefront cafes which are the best feature of that agreeably laid-back town. At another table was another young tourist. We struck up a conversation, in the manner of two people thousands of miles away from their homes at Christmas time. She had just come back from Belize, sixty miles away. I was intending to head into Belize for a side-trip a few days later, and so was interested in what she had to say about that country. She didn't seem interested in talking about her experiences there, however. She was furious that she had had to pay almost US$20 in order to be able to leave Belize. She was on a very tight budget, so this unanticipated expense had made a considerable difference to her. She would probably not be able to afford to visit the spectacular Mayan ruins at Tikal because of it. I was intrigued. Had she committed some minor offence, or was there a problem with her passport which meant that she had

had to bribe a corrupt passport official? No, it seemed that Belize levied an exit tax on foreigners. In fact, the tax has since been raised to $35, payable, for no good reason, only in US dollars, not in Belizian currency.

Exit taxes at land crossings are unusual around the world, and often amount to five dollars at most (see the example below), though some countries levy some form of entry tax. Belize, which marketed itself heavily to tourists and obviously wanted as many people as possible to visit, was simply ensuring that it got a final bite out of each of the 850,000 tourists who visit it each year[1].

As Belize does not allow foreigners to live and work there, travellers have no choice but to pay it, and therefore the tax was little more than legalised extortion. My companion didn't seem to have had any other bad experiences in Belize but this had clearly left a nasty taste in her mouth. I finished my drink, paid the bill and never saw her again.

Most countries let tourists leave them for free, at any rate if they cross their land borders. They may charge you to enter, particularly if you are from a country which needs a visa, but they do not charge you extra to leave. Many countries, however, charge to get out for no obvious reason except to make as much money as possible from travellers. Because travellers have to leave a country to get home, they have to pay the tax. They do not, however, receive any useful service in return, unless you call being able to leave a country a service, and if you do, it is a service which is provided free of charge in the vast majority of countries in the world!

The Belizian charge was not an airport fee of the kind that every customer of an airport must pay each time he or she flies, to fund the airport facilities. My companion in that cafe had left Belize overland. If she had flown out of Belize, she would have paid an airport fee, and IN ADDITION paid the exit tax. The tax is not even levied on everybody who crosses land borders: citizens of Belize, Guatemala and Mexico are exempt, for no good reason. They cross Belize's borders, they use the facilities just as much as other foreigners, but other foreigners pay, and they do not. If the tax were to finance border security, they should surely pay too. But Mexico and Guatemala are poorer countries, and when the tax was first introduced, their citizens had not been able to pay, so they had been stranded in Belize. And Belize citizens, who are not particularly wealthy either, can vote in Belize, so the government never included them in this particular tax, though of course they pay many others. Richer tourists, on the other hand, would always cough up. Some of the charge was earmarked for environmental protection (though it was not obvious why foreigners, who paid the levy, damaged the environment more than Belizians, who were exempt), but most of it fed the Belize government.

There is no obvious way to dodge exit taxes, besides crossing the border illegally, which is not recommended. It often takes you into dangerous territory, and you do not have a passport stamp showing that you left the country, which can complicate things if you want to return. The Central American guidebooks often say that if your Spanish is good enough and you do not mind arguing, you can get out of exit taxes there. I have never heard of anybody being able to dodge it in this way, however, and in most countries it is not possible to dodge the tax. As the sums involved are usually relatively small (between $2-$10 for most countries where I have had to pay an exit tax) this is one of those scams where it is probably better to grit your teeth and pay up.

When I was leaving Belize later on, a Canadian couple in the same bus said that they did not have enough money to pay, and as there were no ATMs at the border and the officials did not take credit cards, they were eventually allowed to leave. There is no guarantee, however, that this will work again. It is, therefore, important to have some money on you, preferably in small bills, in order to be able to pay up.

Selected exit taxes around the world

Exit taxes for tourists who are travelling overland are particularly popular in Central America, a region of the world that has contributed more than its fair share to this collection of scams. The United States charges citizens and green card holders who give up their citizenship an exit tax, and this may be a rip-off, but it is not the subject of this section of the book, as it affects emigrants, rather than tourists. Some examples of exit taxes at the time of writing are:

- Leaving Honduras will cost you around 30 Lempiras ($2), and Nicaragua's exit levy is about the same. It is possible to differentiate between the countries which levy "official" exit taxes, such as Belize, and those which levy "unofficial" exit taxes, such as Nicaragua or Guatemala, where you are in effect the victim of a form of extortion: the passport officials demand a few dollars from you to let you leave. However, this distinction makes little difference to the traveller, who is forced to pay money for no reason by a country whose tourist industry he or she has been supporting.

- Israel and Egypt, too, charge heavy entry and exit taxes for tourists crossing their land borders: at the time of writing, the act of walking from the former to the latter at the frontier town of Taba will cost you around $30/£25.

- Jordanian border guards often sting foreigners for 5 Dinar ($7/£5) when they leave the country, though they apparently forgot or were too lazy to do so when I crossed the border into Israel. All of the dozen people on my bus got through without being charged. However, I met many travellers in Israel who had been forced to pay this levy.

Note:

[1] If each visitor pays the tax, Belize makes around US$15 million/year, or about US$50 for each Belizean, or US$200 for a family of four. Even in a country where the annual income per head is US$8,500, this is a significant amount.

46. Compulsory tourist guide scam

Likely damage: 2/5

Frequency: 1/5

Countries reported: North Korea, Libya, Turkmenistan.

Summary: A few countries still force foreigners to be accompanied by a guide, whether they want him or not.

In many countries, governments require travellers to hire guides to escort them if they are going to particularly dangerous places, often areas of wilderness where death or serious injuries are real possibilities. This is not usually a scam, because the governments concerned do not do this for revenue, but rather for the traveller's safety, and many travellers' lives have doubtless been saved by this practice.

While travelling independently in some countries, visitors (whether tourists or business travellers) have to hire an official guide and companion for their entire stay, even if they do not want one. The guide must remain with them whether they want his services or not, and whether the traveller visits anywhere dangerous or not. This scam used to be a speciality of Communist countries, but with the collapse of Communism since 1989, it is much less common than it used to be.

Today, it is mostly confined to the most repressive countries, such as North Korea. These countries generally receive few tourists in any case, and those that do usually visit them only briefly, and for the bragging rights of having been to one of the most unusual countries on earth.

The guide's job is to stick to the tourist or business traveller like a limpet, knowing where he is and what he is doing at all times. The guide is not a freelance guide whose role is to make sure the tourist has a good time, and who will aim to please, hoping for a large tip at the end of the visit. The main purposes of the guide from the government's point of view are:

- To act as a spy on the traveller. If the traveller photographs something which the government considers sensitive, or even laughs at an inappropriate moment, he is likely to find himself subjected to a furious tirade from the guide. He may even find himself in serious trouble with the police. The traveller can be confident that the guide will file a report on anything he or she says or does with the country's security services. Anything to which the government takes exception can get the traveller into serious trouble.

- To ensure that the traveller does not engage in any activity which the country considers undesirable. This might include telling the locals the truth about their awful government, or going anywhere which the government considers sensitive.

- To ensure that the traveller leaves with as good an impression as possible of the government. Repressive governments have a very low tolerance for anything which can be interpreted as criticism and no sense of humour at all. The guide will almost certainly be a politically trustworthy, and thoroughly indoctrinated, citizen, who will probably spout the government's propaganda at every opportunity. Many awful governments are strangely sensitive about their image overseas, and they want travellers to go home with a favourable impression of their nation.

Needless to say, the traveller is required to pay heavily for the privilege of having a guide who they do not want and who is required to spy on them. Fees in Turkmenistan can be $40-$50 (£25-£30) per day, and in Libya (even post-Gaddafi) or North Korea, they are twice that. Some travellers find their guide's knowledge of local conditions helpful. Those exclusively interested in local history or culture, or in the government's perspective on events, will often enjoy talking to the guide, and getting the regime's perspective on the world, though it is of course important to remember that the government will only tell you what it wants you to hear. Occasionally, of course, something has gone wrong with the government's attempt to control what you see and hear, and the guide is not reliable any more. They may beg for help in getting a visa for the traveller's home country, or for assistance in some form of smuggling. Some masochistic travellers have found trying to dodge the guide an amusing part of a holiday. If they know their way around, and especially if they know the local language well, they can often evade the guide and spend the day seeing the sights and talking to local people.

Despite these possibilities for a positive outcome from this rip-off, it remains a scam. Thousands of travellers who have had guides foisted on them when they have had no interest in what the guide says, and no wish to visit the places to which the guide wants to take them. They have been reported to brutal and unpredictable regimes for trivial offences. The charges for the guides are usually excessive, and any positive results for the traveller are unintended. As with so many governmental scams, however, the only way to avoid paying, unless you are very good at negotiating, is not to visit the country at all.

Compulsory state-sponsored guide in North Korea

The current cost for this service in North Korea is $100/day – a lot for most single travellers, and many times the average daily wage in North Korea. Countries where this scam has been reported tend to be desperate for hard currency, and even $100/day from the few tourists which North Korea receives is a useful source of revenue.

47. "Official" exchange rates

Likely damage: 2/5

Frequency: 1/5

Countries reported: Venezuela, Cuba, most of Africa, much of Central Asia.

Summary: Tourists have to exchange money at a ridiculous exchange rate in many countries, just so the government can get its hands on foreign currency.

In the 1970s and 1980s, many Communist countries had two exchange rates: one for "official transactions", and one for tourism and similar purposes. The government would always force travellers to use the least favourable rate when changing their money. Twenty years after Communism collapsed, this scam continues in a few countries. It is clearly a swindle: travellers are being forced to pay far over the odds for local money, for no reason other than to benefit the government of the country to which they travel. The black market which always grows up is sometimes tolerated, and sometimes it is savagely persecuted, but no country with two or more exchange rates has ever succeeded in stamping it out.

This is one scam where the rules, and the best means of avoiding it, vary from country to country. In some countries, the rules are enforced so strictly that the financial gain from changing money on the black market simply is not worth the risk of being caught. As so often when breaking the law in a foreign country, you are extremely vulnerable to blackmail by criminals or extortion by the police (see scam #61), and at worst could face a lengthy prison sentence. In other countries, the black market in foreign exchange is tolerated. It is therefore much better to research the exact situation in the country before you travel, and always be cautious when deciding where and how to change your money.

Two Communist countries scam my family with terrible exchange rates

On Sunday 12 November 1989, when I was very young, my father took us on a day trip to Berlin. We were curious to see the then-communist East before it disintegrated completely. It turned out to be an incredible day trip because, the previous Thursday, the East German government had announced that all East German citizens were free to visit the West for the first time in decades. It had in effect demolished the Berlin Wall.

We arrived at the airport in Berlin, and took the bus and then the subway to the nearest East German station, where you could access the East. We stopped at the rather sinister immigration checkpoint, and handed our passports to the frontier guard. He gave us visas after some delay but without any difficulty. He then demanded 25 Deutsche Marks each, or 75 Deutsche Marks in total, from us. We protested that we did not want to stay more than an hour or so in the East, and did not want to spend any money there.

The guard clearly enjoyed telling us, however, that foreigners visiting East Germany had to buy 25 Ostmarks (the currency in the East) each at an exchange rate of 1:1 for each day that they intended to stay in East Germany. Needless to say, we would have to keep them; we would not be able to change them back when we left the country. My father knew better than to argue with an East German border guard, especially given the memorial we had just seen to the refugees they had shot since the Wall was built, so he handed over the Deutsche Marks. We consoled ourselves with the thought that the Ostmarks would at least make souvenirs, albeit rather expensive ones.

We were to have a similar experience when we visited the Soviet Union the following year. We changed our foreign currency into roubles at an exchange rate of one rouble per US dollar, when we could have got five or six times as many roubles for the same amount of foreign currency on the black market, had we trusted one of the numerous touts who swarmed around our hotel. Changing at the official exchange rate made Russia a fairly expensive country, while changing it at the black market rate made it extremely cheap. (Of course, given the chronic shortages in the Soviet Union at the time, spending the roubles we had bought was another matter …)

Countries with dual exchange rates today

Countries with dual exchange rates are much rarer than they used to be. However, the governments of some countries, mostly in Africa and Central Asia, still force travellers to change money at outrageously unfavourable exchange rates.

Communist Cuba has two parallel currencies: the convertible peso and the local peso. The exchange rate is 24:1. Most basic goods, such as fruit and vegetables, are priced in local pesos. Most goods a tourist is likely to buy, however, are priced in convertible pesos. In areas frequented by tourists, many shops have price tags which do not specify the currency. Tourists who pay in convertible pesos for a good price in local pesos, are paying 24 times as much as they should pay. Local shopkeepers rarely point out that mistake.

The Bolivarian Republic of Venezuela has maintained strict currency controls since 2003 and in November 2016 a legal exchange rate of 658 bolivars per dollar was used for tourists at ATMs. On the black market, where people and businesses turn when they cannot obtain government approval to purchase dollars at the legal rates, the bolivar was trading at 1,567 bolivars per dollar in November 2016. On the border with Colombia, the rate was even weaker at 1,737.50 bolivars per dollar.

Scammers at the Thai/Cambodian border

At some borders, crooks will pretend that the law says that you have to change money with them at an unfavourable exchange rate, when you do not. Cambodian scammers at the border with Thailand sometimes insist that travellers change $50/£40 or $100/£80, even when you are not required to do so. They may pretend that there are no ATMs in Cambodia, when there are actually plenty in Phnom Penh, Siem Reap and other towns.

Chapter 8: E-mail and Internet scams

In the two decades that the Internet has been widely used, it has revolutionised many aspects of travelling. Anybody with a credit card can book flights without calling or visiting a travel agent or airline; travellers can keep in touch with home much more easily; and they can easily obtain virtually unlimited amounts of information. It has made travelling so much easier that, today, taking all but the simplest package holiday is inconceivable without using the Internet.

While it is a great help to most travellers the majority of the time, it is also a happy hunting ground for crooks. The FBI in the United States reports double-digit rates of growth for cybercrime and Scotland Yard in Britain estimates that online fraud is worth tens of billions of pounds each year worldwide. A significant proportion of this comes from travellers.

48. Internet cafes and internet banking scams

Likely damage: 3/5

Frequency: 1/5

Countries reported: Venezuela, Brazil, Bolivia, Thailand, South Africa.

Summary: How tourists' bank account details can be stolen at Internet cafes.

Using the Internet on your own laptop or smartphone while travelling is becoming easier all the time, but in some places, it is still necessary, or at least most convenient, to use an Internet cafe, and that makes people vulnerable to a number of scams. Perhaps the most worrying and pernicious, and the most difficult to detect, preys on travellers who access their bank accounts at an Internet cafe. Before the Internet became so widespread, travellers could only contact their bank at home with an inconvenient and expensive phone call, and often then only at inconvenient times (try calling a European bank during banking hours from Australia). Now, it is easy to contact a bank online. All banks require customers accessing their accounts online to enter login names and one or more passwords. They can then check their balances, transfer funds, pay bills, dispute transactions and so on.

Crooks have not been slow to exploit Internet banking:

A few Internet cafes have installed CCTV or "spyware"[1] to monitor the customers' keystrokes as they type in their details.

In other Internet cafes, criminals may scam travellers in the following way:

1. Crooks who have nothing to do with the management of the business take advantage of lax security policies there to install spyware.

2. Once they have the customers' logins and passwords, it is relatively simple for the scammers to raid the customers' bank accounts, transferring funds out to accounts they control, ordering money transfers which they then pick up or buying marketable goods from eBay. Banks try to prevent unusual transactions to some extent by freezing customers' accounts if they spot odd activity, but their software cannot spot every attempted fraud[2].

3. The traveller will only detect the scam once he realises that his bank account has been emptied.

4. It could, however, take several days or a week before he next has access to an ATM and realises that his bank has blocked his account. It will probably take even longer, and several phone calls to the bank back home, before the traveller begins to realise what has happened.

5. Even then, pinning it on the criminals at the Internet cafe will be very difficult, if not impossible.

6. The traveller may get his money back eventually, depending on the laws in his home country, and how customer-friendly his bank is, but it can be a complex and stressful process.

7. If the traveller has bills falling due and no money to meet them, his credit score can be badly affected as an indirect consequence of having his account raided in this way.

These scams are becoming increasingly common, and, in response, banks' online security is more and more elaborate and difficult to crack. Some, for instance, demand an answer from a question in a set list of questions which scammers attempting to access the account are unlikely to know (what is your mother's maiden name? How old was your father when you were born?). There is no need to be paranoid when using an Internet cafe, or to stop using them altogether, to avoid becoming a victim of fraud. Nevertheless, there are ways to make it less likely that you will be ripped off in this way:

- When using the Internet in a public place, it is important to refuse if the computer offers to let you store your user name and password. Most banks' software does not allow passwords to be stored in this way in any case, though e-mail sites such as Hotmail do not have this protection.

- Changing passwords and, if possible, logins every so often is also a good idea, particularly when travelling, though most banks advise their customers to do so in any case, and most customers (including me) are rather bad at following their advice.

- When typing in a password or PIN in an Internet café, it is more secure to shield the hand which is doing the typing, so that the keystrokes cannot be seen, either by other people using the computers or by any CCTV which the cafe has installed.

- Finally, in order to detect fraud, it is a good idea to check bank balances and account transactions at least every week or so, even at the risk of using another Internet cafe which might steal your passwords. In fact, it is a good idea to do this in any case, as foreign scammers are not the only people who try to access people's bank accounts and steal their hard earned cash.

Risks of using free public wifi

More and more airports, cities, hotels and other places around the world provide free wifi. However, in 2016, a report by AVG Technologies argued that it was relatively easy for scammers to set up wifi that mimicked free public networks. Users' data could then be stolen as they used the fake networks. This could be particularly dangerous if the victims used the networks for internet banking or online purchases. The report made various recommendations for customers to be safe. These included making purchases using a secure payment method (https:// *not* http://) and ensuring that login passwords and accounts used for bank accounts are not the same as those used for social media.

South African internet banking spyware scam busted

In July 2005, South African police arrested a man and confiscated computer equipment in Johannesburg. They found spyware installed on 13 public computers in Internet cafes and other public computers. It had been used to capture customers' Internet banking account numbers, passwords and other details. American, Canadian and English tourists visiting South Africa were among the 50 or so customers who had had their accounts looted of tens of thousands of dollars in total.

Notes:

[1] "Spyware" is software which makes it possible for criminals to record people's keystrokes, in this case, Internet banking logins and passwords.

[2] In any case a blocked account when travelling is a major headache for the customer in itself – I recall arriving in Cusco, Peru from Bolivia with no cash or travellers cheques, thinking that I would be able to withdraw money from my bank account at an ATM. I hired a taxi with another traveller, and told him to take me to the nearest bank. Unfortunately, my bank had for some reason thought that my withdrawing money and paying for hotel rooms in Bolivia had been unusual, and had blocked my account. Fortunately, my travelling companion had enough money to pay for the taxi, but it was still an awkward moment, as I had to depend on the good nature of somebody I had only just met. The phone lines between Cusco and my home town must have melted as I called my bank and demanded that they let me get at my own money again.

49. Attack website and malicious spam scams

Likely damage: 3/5

Frequency: 2/5

Countries reported: Global.

Summary: Scammers use fake websites and email attachments promising travel tickets to steal travellers' credit card details.

Many people now buy airline tickets from online travel agents' websites. Legitimate sites such as Skyscanner.net and Lastminute.com allow travellers to compare prices of airline tickets between different airlines and choose the best value. Travellers can save a lot of time and money by buying airline tickets from such websites rather than the airlines direct, though airlines sometimes encourage tourists to buy tickets from their sites. For instance, a tourist who buys a cheap economy ticket directly from British Airways' or Virgin Atlantic's site can change the date for a fee, instead of having to buy a new ticket if his or her travel plans change.

Unfortunately, not all travel agents' websites are legitimate:

- Some take their victims' money and credit card details and do not supply them with tickets (see scam #26). Others, however, are "attack websites": sites which install malicious software (so-called "malware") on their victims' computers. This can then record their credit card information or internet banking passwords, or it can allow them to take over computers and send spam to other victims.

- Other fraudulent websites pretend to offer airline tickets. When their victims try to buy, the sites record their credit card numbers, expiry dates, security codes, names and addresses and use them to raid their credit card accounts (see the example below). Though the victims' credit cards are valid, the site will show them a screen saying that the site cannot process it, and so they will not receive the tickets they think they are buying. A short time later, the scammers may even attempt to rob the victim again, by calling him and trying to get him to wire them money for the tickets.

There are ways to spot which travel agency websites are fraudulent and which are genuine:

- Simply doing an Internet search for the website's name with "scam" or "fraud" (such as typing "XXXX Travel Agency scam" without the quotation marks into your search engine) may turn up accusations of fraud.

- Poor spelling or grammar on the website may also mean that the people behind the site are amateur criminals rather than professional travel agents.

- Another sign which should set off alarm bells is very low prices. The online travel agency business is very competitive, and deals which seem much better than all their competitors' offerings may well be fraudulent.

There are also some tips to protect against the "malware" – software which attack websites or spammers try to install on their victims' computers to steal their personal financial information. The United States Computer Emergency Readiness Team (US-CERT) is the part of the Department of Homeland Security which combats threats from computer viruses. It recommends:

- Having up-to-date virus protection and a firewall will block some attacks, depending on the security settings.

- If you receive an unsolicited email from an unknown source, never open any attachments or respond to any requests for your financial details.

E-mail airline ticket scam #1

US-CERT has identified a number of scams which target people buying airline tickets. In one of them, on which US-CERT reported in 2008 (but still relevant today), the scammers send an unsolicited email, which appears to come from a legitimate airline. They attach a zip file, which is disguised as an invoice and ticket:

- The subject line was "E-Ticket#XXXXXXXXXX"

- An attachment was named "eTicket#XXXX.zip"

If the user opens the attachment, it installs malicious code onto her computer. The victim's computer may then be taken over by the scammers.

E-mail airline ticket scam #2

A similar scam to that in the example above was reported by the anti-virus firm Sophos in 2009. Emails purporting to come from Northwest or United Airlines were sent to passengers, with attachments called "Your_ETicket.zip". Again, downloading the attachment installed a virus on the victims' computers' which stole their personal data.

It followed spam disguised as an email message from US-Customs with an attachment, entitled "Bill_Tax.zip", with the same characteristics.

50. eBay holiday scams

Likely damage: 3/5

Frequency: 2/5

Countries reported: Global.

Summary: Fraudsters sell people worthless travel-related goods on eBay and vanish with their money.

Many travel-related goods can be bought cheaper on eBay than from travel agents. Cutting out the middle-man and the associated advertising costs can save money, and I am one of the many who has saved thousands buying goods, both travel-related and otherwise, on eBay over the years. eBay has a good reputation for cracking down on fraudsters once it investigates them. Negative feedback from sellers about buyers who have swindled them in the past is available on the site for everybody to read. Fraud on eBay concerning travel-related products is nevertheless a real problem. It goes further than the relatively specific scam in which scammers book a refundable ticket, sell it and cancel it. eBay scams are relatively simple for a fraudster to organise. For example:

- The scammer will advertise a product for sale on eBay, perhaps a package tour or a cruise, at a low, but not exceptionally low, price. He may use photographs from a legitimate company's website.

- The scammer will then ask his victims to send payment for the products to his PayPal account.

- The scammer will withdraw the money in cash. He may or may not send the victims worthless, faked "tickets".

- When they turn up to the airport or the cruise ship, the victims will find that they have not booked a holiday and they will be most unlikely ever to see their money again.

Another classic eBay scam is the "second chance auction" scam:

1. A bidder has come second in a legitimate eBay auction for a cruise or some tickets to an event.

2. Scammers will note the bidder's eBay name and what he bid. They may be able to guess his email address since many users use the first part of their email address (say johnsmith) as their eBay ID.

3. They send unsolicited email to addresses composed of the eBay ID at common domain names (such as johnsmith@hotmail.com, johnsmith@yahoo.com, johnsmith@gmail.com and so on) hoping to reach the unsuccessful bidder.

4. They will offer him the same product for a slightly lower price than what he was willing to pay. They will ask him to send the money through Western Union, or some other relatively untraceable method.

5. If the victim sends the money, they will not send him the product promised, and the victim will never see his money again.

In order to check whether the travel-related product you are buying on eBay is likely to be legitimate:

- It is worth bearing in mind the common saying that, "if something looks too good to be true, it probably is". Auctions which offer unrealistically large savings may well be fraudulent.

- At the time of writing, much international eBay fraud seems to come from Romania, so it is wise to be sceptical of any auctions which involve users who seem to be in that country.

- In addition, eBay shows feedback for each seller from previous buyers under their user names and it is always advisable to check to see what previous buyers have said.

- eBay accounts can be hijacked. If the account has been offering car parts for years, and suddenly starts offering Caribbean cruises, this could be a sign that the original account holder is no longer in control.

- Another warning sign is if somebody who has been a buyer in most auctions previously is now a seller. Most people who act in this way are legitimate sellers, but, it is another yellow flag, which, taken in combination with other warnings, can add up to a red flag.

Australian teenager convicted of eBay fraud

Joash Boyton was 19 when he began defrauding people. In 2011 and 2012 Boyton used stolen credit-card numbers to buy airline tickets and household goods which he then sold on auction websites, or employed others to sell on his behalf. His scams became so complex that Victoria Police's e-crimes squad had to investigate for more than two years. One victim was in Europe when she found out that her tickets were worthless, effectively stranding her. Boyton was sentenced to almost five years in jail.

Man arrested for eBay fraud

In 2011, a man from Liverpool was arrested in the UK for taking holiday bookings worth thousands of pounds through eBay. The police alleged that he would make the bookings on behalf of his clients, then cancel them, without refunding customers' money.

51. Travel-related spam scams

Likely damage: 3/5

Frequency: 2/5

Countries reported: Global, in particular Thailand, Russia, Ukraine, Nigeria.

Summary: Scammers swindle their victims using spam e-mails.

Unsolicited marketing e-mail, or spam, is almost always annoying and often fraudulent. Most people delete it unread, though apparently, as e-mails are usually free or very cheap to send, enough people respond to make it worthwhile to continue to send them[1]. Most frauds which use e-mail are relatively easy to spot, and many customers of webmail services delete dozens of such e-mails each month. Some scam e-mails, however, are more convincing, especially if they seem to come from people whom the victim knows and trusts, and a few of these scams disproportionately or specifically target travellers. They may ask for financial information such as money or credit card details.

In another e-mail scam:

1. The male victim is lured overseas, either by spam e-mail or by a website promising cheap gems or a beautiful bride.

2. The e-mails invite him to fly to a foreign country to seal the deal, and collect the valuables.

3. If the victim is buying gems, he will be told to bring cash.

4. He is met by the scammers at the airport, and at some point he is mugged and all his valuables are taken. He may even be kidnapped and held for ransom.

Many other e-mail scams which target travellers also involve the booming business of international dating. Many travellers to some countries, such as Russia or Thailand, are men in search of local brides. Hundreds of online agencies have sprung up in the last decade to make such matches and help the resulting couples with visa and other problems. Some are legitimate, but many are not. Even those that are above-board can attract scammers. Some scam prospective husbands in the following way:

1. The victim meets a woman online and gets on very well with the female scammer.

2. The victim agrees to travel to her country and see her.

3. In fact, their first and only date is at a luxury shopping mall, where he is put under intense pressure to buy her expensive goods. He does so, they have a romantic dinner, for which he also pays.

4. He calls her the next day to meet up again, but cannot get through.

5. He never hears from her again.

Another scam connected with online dating works as follows:

1. The website of the agency posts a picture of a beautiful woman.

2. A victim pays the agency for her contact details.

3. An e-mail or letter mail exchange begins. The victim believes that he is writing to the woman in the picture, while he is in fact writing to scammers.

4. After a while, the scammers ask their victim for money. They may pretend that the woman needs cash to buy a computer for "her" home so that "she" can e-mail him more regularly. "She" may say that "she" needs cash for a plane ticket and visa fees so that "she" can visit him.

5. The victim will send the money, and never see it again.

One way of spotting scammers on online dating sites is to ask for a phone number. "Women" on dating sites who are actually scammers will usually refuse to give a phone number, or give an invalid one, to the victim.

The usual advice with dealing with any form of spam is that:

- E-mails from unknown companies should be with treated with extreme suspicion, and, even if you do know the company, check that the website and e-mail are theirs.

- E-mails that seem to be from scammers can be reported to the appropriate authorities or simply ignored.

- Do not contact anyone listed on the e-mail, and never give out any personal information, such as bank account information or even your date of birth.

- NEVER pay any fees of any kind in response to unsolicited emails.

- Do not cash any cheques from someone who has sent you spam, as they are very likely to be fraudulent, and never give them cash on the strength of a cheque, even if it has already cleared in your account. The cheque is probably forged and will almost certainly bounce several weeks later. You will be held liable for the money you have sent them.

Internet café/e-mail scam

An example of an unscrupulous e-mail scam of this type was sent to me by a traveller in Africa. Unlike most e-mail scams, the scammer needs to be in the same place as the person he targets:

1. The scammer will hang out in an internet café, and stare unobtrusively at people's screens after they have left.

2. The scammer will try and find a computer whose previous user (call her "Rebecca") has forgotten to log out of their e-mail.

3. The scammer will then sit at the computer and use the open e-mail account to send e-mails to Rebecca's contacts, such as her

parents or friends. The e-mail will say that Rebecca has had her passport, travel tickets and luggage stolen. It will try to give a convincing impression of stress and urgency. It will say that she needs money wired to an account in the city where the Internet café is.

4. The good-natured, but now worried, parents or friends may well send the money asked, especially if the sum involved is not too large. The account is controlled by the scammer, who will pocket any money sent, close the account and then vanish.

As with some of the most pernicious scams, this one plays on people's good nature and concern for friends or relatives overseas.

A similar scam has been reported as working through Facebook. If a scammer can get the password to a Facebook account, either by watching a victim type it in, or by using a virus to record his details, he can change it and lock his victim out. He can then send messages to the victim's Facebook friends begging for money to be wired to his victim, to an account which he specifies.

Note:

[1] A list of the most common cyber scams is available on the FBI's website at https://www.fbi.gov/investigate/cyber

52. "International Driving Licences" scam

Likely damage: 3/5

Frequency: 2/5

Countries reported: Global.

Summary: Worthless clones of International Driver's Permits are sold online by scammers who pretend that they have some validity.

Travellers who want to drive in foreign countries should check exactly what documentation they will need before they leave home. It is sometimes possible to do so on your home country's driving licence; European Union countries, for instance, recognise each other's driving licences, so a Frenchman can drive in Greece and a Spaniard in Germany without a problem. Citizens of English-speaking countries can use their English language licences in the United States, providing they are not resident there. Most other countries, however, require travellers to buy an International Driver's Permit (IDP) in their home country, which they can do on production of their driving licences for a small charge.

There is considerable confusion and misinformation about what an IDP will let its owner do. It is proof that he holds a valid driving licence in his home country at the date of issue. It will NOT let its owner drive anywhere he would not be able to drive otherwise. If the owner is banned from driving in his home country, it will NOT let him drive overseas. It will no longer be valid when the owner's driving licence expires. It is only a translation of his existing licence into the five official United Nations languages (English, Spanish, French, Russian and Chinese), to enable police and anybody else with a reason to do so (such as car rental companies) to read the important information (name, date of birth and so on) on the licence.

Most countries which issue IDPs control who can issue them tightly:

- In the United States, only two organisations are allowed to issue IDPs, the American Automobile Association and the American Automobile Touring Alliance's National Automobile Club.

- In Australia, the state governments and automobile associations may issue them.

- In Canada, the Canadian Automobile Association is the only body which can issue them.

- In the United Kingdom, the Royal Automobile Club and the Automobile Association are allowed to issue them.

These organisations usually charge a small fee, perhaps $10/£6, for the IDP.

It is best to buy an IDP from these legitimate organisations. However, scammers have seen several opportunities to make money from the fact that most people do not know exactly what an IDP is, or what it is for, but always vaguely associate it with travelling. These scams are usually conducted by unsolicited e-mails or websites. One common scam is similar to a scam involving free visas (see scam #27).

1. The swindlers advertise an IDP for a substantial fee, perhaps $50-80/£40-£70, well in excess of the cost of the original IDP.

2. The victim will be asked for his details and eventually will be sent a document in the post.

3. This document will simply be an IDP obtained (but at greater expense to the victim) from the legitimate organisation which issues them.

The profit from this scam can be $50/£40 per IDP sold.

In another scam involving permits for international driving:

1. The scammers may offer and supply an International Driving Licence (IDL), Official International Driving Permit, or something similar, to people who are likely to mistake it for an IDP.

2. The scammers will, of course, make the usual excessive charge, and demand their victim's details. They may claim that their document is useful as identification, or that it entitles their victims to drive where they would not otherwise be able to drive. They may claim that it will allow their victims to drive overseas while they are banned in their home country. They may even claim that the IDL can never be suspended or revoked.

3. The document that they send is essentially worthless – simply a translation of their victim's current licence into a number of foreign languages. It will be similar to the IDP, but much more expensive and without its official character.

These IDLs can, in fact, be dangerous to the victim of the scam, and many governments and motoring organisations have issued warnings not to buy or use them (see examples below).

To avoid being a victim of this scam:

- Do not answer any of the spam that offers these licences, no matter how legitimate the organisation sending the mail seems to be.

- Instead, buy an International Driver's Permit from the organisations which are allowed to sell them by your government. The cost of doing so will probably be far less, and the IDP will be valid in the 150 countries around the world where it is recognised.

- Remember that the point of an IDP is not to act as a substitute for your home driver's licence, but only to act as a translation, so that law enforcement officials in the country to which you are going can read it in case you break the law or are involved in an accident. When you expect to drive overseas, *always bring* your home driver's licence with you as well as your IDP.

US government warning about IDPs

The United States Department of State has the following warning on its website: "The Department of State is aware that IDPs are being sold over the Internet and in person by persons not authorized by the Department of State pursuant to the requirements of the U.N. Convention of 1949. Moreover, many of these IDPs are being sold for large sums of money, far greater than the sum charged by entities authorized by the Department of State. Consumers experiencing problems should report problems to their local office of the U.S. Postal Inspector, the Better Business Bureau, or their state or local Attorney General's Office".

South African Automobile Association warns about fake travel permits

In 2006, the South African Automobile Association warned that: "We are aware that many drivers may unwittingly use this illegal international driving licence without realising the consequences. They could be seriously compromised should they be involved in an accident without a valid South African driving licence and international driving permit. It is also almost impossible to hire a car abroad without a valid international permit".

Goan police target tourists on motorbikes without IDPs

I have heard from several sources that the Goan police have been demanding "on the spot fines", i.e. bribes, from foreign tourists who hire motorcycles without the required IDPs. While the fines are rarely huge, usually $20-30, being stopped and quizzed by the police can be a traumatic experience, and those that cannot or refuse to pay can be taken to jail.

Chapter 9: Begging and street hustling scams

Most travellers come from relatively wealthy countries where there are plenty of jobs which provide most people with comparatively decent wages. Confronting the extreme poverty suffered by many in countries like Egypt or India can therefore be an unpleasant shock, especially as it is such a great contrast to the natural or architectural beauty advertised in the tourist brochures. These are countries in which a secure job with a decent living is a distant dream to the overwhelming majority of the inhabitants.

Not knowing where one's next meal is coming from is often just a figure of speech in the West, but is literally true for billions of people around the world. Being orphaned or disabled, mentally or physically in poorer countries, usually means a lifetime of dependence on other people's unpredictable charity. It can even mean death by starvation. Many people who would not give money to beggars at home therefore feel that they should do so in poorer countries.

Many travellers find extreme poverty amongst young children the most distressing aspect of life in poorer countries. Child beggars are commonplace, and are often forced by adults to demand money from strangers to get anything to eat at all.

53. Begging

Likely damage: 1/5

Frequency: 4/5

Countries reported: Global.

Summary: Gangs of panhandlers prey on travellers' generosity. Beggars fake injuries to get greater donations.

The unscrupulous can exploit both the poverty of their vulnerable fellow citizens and the generosity of travellers towards those helpless people. Beggars often scam travellers by giving them something of little value, such as a flower, and expecting a donation of money in return. They can also claim to have found something on the ground, such as a book or a piece of jewellery, and give it to their victim. They can then demand money and follow their victim until he obliges, and since they will usually be happy with a few pennies, the victim may think it will be easier to give in to their demands than to continue refusing.

One of the oldest scams related to begging, perhaps best known from its depiction in Charles Dickens's Oliver Twist, is the begging gang. This practice is most common in poor countries, but is also a growing problem in Western Europe:

1. A gang master will recruit children, the disabled or the very old, and teach them how to coax or steal money from tourists.

2. He will demand all of their takings, and in return give them only enough food to keep them alive.

3. He will often keep them in line with physical abuse (see the example below).

4. He may underfeed them or ply them with drugs so that they look sad, and therefore seem more pitiable to tourists or others.

5. He may also train some of them to pick pockets while others distract tourists.

The beggars will often go along with this because of the minimal sense of security it provides, and out of a misplaced sense of loyalty to their master. If they are children they may not know any different way of life. Sometimes the "recruiting" actually takes the form of kidnapping children likely to be good as beggars from their families, and occasionally parents even sell their children into this form of slavery. By giving money to child beggars, a tourist could be supporting any of these practises.

It is not only street beggars who may attempt to scam travellers. People who appear to be collecting money for charity may actually be collecting it for themselves, particularly in developed countries:

1. The scammers may approach a traveller, give a token such as a plastic flower or a card with writing on it and then demand money.

2. Often, they will carry dozens of such gifts, and hand them out to all the people in a restaurant, or sitting in a part. They may mention a well-known charity, and they will demand money from their victims.

3. Typically, if they are attempting to scam someone by mentioning a charity with which they have no connection, they will go away if asked for ID, which most legitimate charity collectors carry.

4. They will keep any money which they receive.

Disabled beggars can also scam travellers. People will occasionally mutilate themselves, or, horrifyingly, their children deliberately to stimulate pity and so earn more money. Beggars with open wounds will deliberately keep them open for the same reason. Giving money to disabled beggars, therefore, can have the effect of encouraging this horrific practice, which also makes it much more difficult for the beggar ever to have a regular job again.

The frequent advice to travellers who want to reduce poverty is to make a donation to any of the many charities who work with these people, such as Care International, Save the Children or Oxfam. Giving an article such as food or clothing can be a better way to reduce poverty than giving money to a beggar.

Travellers usually suffer from these scams much less than the beggars themselves, who are the victims of the desperate poverty in their own countries or of exploitation by unscrupulous gang masters. Travellers are, however, an essential part of this scam. They are victims in the sense that their money is not relieving poverty in the way that they intended.

Chinese beggar gangs investigated

In 2014, the South China Morning Post reported on beggar gangs in China. Its article makes horrific reading. Criminal gangs in the Guangdong industry hub of Dongguan would enslave large numbers of physically disabled children, and force them to work as beggars on the street. The gangs would keep the children in captivity, provide only minimum rations to keep them alive, and pocket any money earned by the children as beggars. In extreme cases, they would even cripple healthy young children to elicit more sympathy from passers-by.

Vietnamese couple arrested for smuggling beggars into Thailand

In 2010, a Vietnamese couple, living in Thailand, were charged with recruiting ten disabled people over three years to beg and sell trinkets in Bangkok. Each recruit paid the couple 300 Baht ($9/£7)/day and kept whatever they made. The Thai police advised people not to give money to beggars.

Pakistani boy's arm broken to make him beg better

In 2008, Pakistani police, searching for a kidnap victim, arrested a begging gang. An eight-year-old boy told them that one of the gang masters had broken his arm. He and his fellow beggars would be placed at good begging locations and made to beg. The money was collected by the gang masters who kept the children alive and begging in return.

54. Parisian gold ring scam

Likely damage: 1/5

Frequency: 2/5

Countries reported: Europe.

Summary: A girl drops a fake gold ring in front of a tourist and tries to persuade him to buy it for far more than it is worth.

Some specific scams are so common they deserve specific coverage in a section of their own. One of these is the gold ring scam, which is so common in Paris, and hardly known elsewhere. Each time I have travelled through Paris, I have met a few people who have been scammed in this way, and the Internet has many reports of this trick. In outline, it is extremely simple:

1. The victim is strolling in a touristy area of Paris, or sitting in a Parisian café with a glass of wine and a Croque Monsieur. He does not notice the young girl in front of him, in suitably pitiful clothes, and is approached by a young girl.

2. The young girl is a scammer. She is walking towards him, and suddenly starts squealing. The victim cannot help but look at her, and make eye contact.

3. The scammer bends down and seems to pick something up from the street. She shows it to her victim. It is a gold ring, or at least a gold-coloured ring. "It is my lucky day", she says in broken English, "look at what I have found. I love gold jewellery. I was hoping to buy something like this, and now I have found one. Is it not beautiful?"

4. The scammer looks so happy that the victim cannot help feeling for her. He answers that it is indeed beautiful and that it must indeed be her lucky day.

5. Now comes the scam. Her face falls. "Ah, unfortunately, I may need to sell it. I have not eaten in the last day, and I need to buy some bread. How much would you say it is worth?" she asks. She hands it to the victim.

6. The victim is not an expert jeweller, but just wants to say something to keep her happy and hopefully get rid of her. He tells her that it is worth €10 (£8/$1210), and then hands it back to her. Then she hands it back to him, saying that she should actually pass her luck on to him, to make it his lucky day. Wouldn't he like to help her eat? He said it was worth €10. Would he begrudge somebody who is starving the chance to sell her last valuable possession and buy some bread? She will go on like this for a long time, until the victim's resistance is worn down.

7. Her objective may be to make him feel bad and buy the ring, which is in fact completely worthless. Or she may hope that the victim will get bored with arguing over the matter, and pay her €10 just to get rid of her.

This scam, therefore, combines misrepresentation of the value of a piece of jewellery with aggressive begging to get some money from a traveller. It can be the cover for something more sinister if the scammer has an accomplice. While she is talking to the victim, and distracting his attention, her accomplice can steal from him, if he has a wallet in his pocket or a handbag, or if he is are sitting at a table with a camera on it.

A variation on this scam has been reported from some countries in Europe, including France and Italy:

1. The victim is in one of the main squares of a large European city.

2. A scammer approaches him and ties a friendship bracelet on the victim's wrist.

3. The scammer demands some money, say €20 (£17/$22), from the victim.

4. If the victim does not want to pay up, the scammer asks for his bracelet back. Unfortunately, the bracelet is tied too tightly around the victim's wrist for him to be able to return it.

5. The victim may, therefore, feel guilty enough to give the scammer his €20, or may become annoyed and rip it off, in which case the scammer will claim some "compensation".

6. The victim can simply say "no" repeatedly and walk off with the bracelet, but these scammers can be very persistent.

Sometimes the scammer will tie a string around the victim's wrist to make a friendship bracelet, but leave a piece of string connected to the bracelet in his hand, so that the victim is in effect tied to him. This can feel very threatening, particularly if the scammer is a large man and the victim is a small woman. Most men who scam in this way are not violent, and are unlikely to assault their victims, though it is always possible that any victim can be unlucky. However, many have complained that the police are unlikely to be able to do much. The scammers are persistent and play on the victim's desire to avoid confrontation and his or her fear of being rude.

There are, however, a number of ways in which you can avoid becoming a victim once you realise what is going on:

- You can pretend not to speak English when you are approached, answering any queries in a foreign language or in a made-up language of your own.

- You can also simply tell the scammer "No", repeatedly, and hopefully they will choose another target.

- You can pick a low value for the ring or bracelet, say ten cents, and hope that the scammer will decide that it is not worth continuing the conversation. They may, however, simply try to convince you to raise your estimate (though in practice, your much lower estimate will probably be much closer to its real value than theirs).

- You can simply refuse to hand over any money when you are asked. And you can say that you have no need for a gold ring of the kind offered.

55. Baksheesh scams

Likely damage: 1/5

Frequency: 5/5

Countries reported: Global.

Summary: Hustlers demand money for providing no obvious services.

"Baksheesh", in its various English spellings, is an Arabic word with no direct equivalent in English or most other European languages. It essentially conveys the idea of giving someone a tip, but does not mean that they necessarily provide a service, and certainly not one which you actually want, in exchange. It can include elements of paying a bribe and rewarding a beggar, though any suggestion that you consider that the people who demand baksheesh are beggars would cause great offence.

While the word may not be familiar to English speakers, however, the practices which it embodies are well known to virtually everybody who has travelled in the Middle East, and many other poorer countries too. Touts who demand baksheesh can congregate anywhere, but are often found in the arrivals section of airports; where buses arrive; in hotel lobbies and around famous tourist attractions such as the Taj Mahal or the Pyramids.

Hustlers like the old Moroccan or the Fijian wood carvers in the examples below exist all over the world, especially in poorer countries.

- I have been steered into unwanted visits to carpet shops in Turkey, hammock stalls in Mexico and hotels in a number of countries.

- In Istanbul, shoe shine boys drop brushes in front of their victims. When the victims point out that the shoe shine boy has dropped his brush, the boy will offer them a free shoeshine and harangue them into giving them a big tip.

- I was faced by a long queue at an airline check-in desk in Caracas airport in Venezuela, when an official appeared unasked for at my side and escorted me to the front of the queue. He did not mention an upfront charge for this service, but needless to say, when he was about to leave me, he demanded $10/£8, which he quickly reduced to $5/£4. Like most people, I do not enjoy standing in line, so I felt that it was money well spent, but a more patient traveller, or a tourist on a tighter budget, would have objected.

Many of these countries where baksheesh is a way of life have fine traditions of hospitality to strangers, which these touts pervert to make money. It is interesting to travel to Jordan, in the Middle East, and contrast the genuine warmth and friendliness of people in most of the country with the shameless, high pressure hustlers in and around the great tourist attraction of Petra. Most Jordanians are polite, friendly and genuinely out to help, while the touts around Petra are just out to get as much of their victims' money as possible with the minimum effort.

Places with a particularly bad reputation for baksheesh include Morocco, Egypt and India. The touts make a precarious living by preying on the openness and good nature of most travellers, together with their tiredness and disorientation when they arrive at a new town. They talk their way into providing unwanted services which the travellers did not ask for, but are too polite to refuse. They rarely mention in advance that they will charge for their services, but there IS always a charge at the end, even if it is sometimes hidden in the price paid for a hotel to which one is firmly steered.

People are sometimes deterred from visiting countries where this kind of hassle is particularly bad. While this is understandable, it is also a shame, as Egypt and India, for example, have sights and attractions which should delight even the most jaded traveller. Travellers can take various steps to avoid paying too much baksheesh:

- Refusing to make eye contact with people whom you suspect will hassle you makes them more likely to choose another victim.

- Being very clear from the outset that you have no intention of paying any money to your new "friend" is also helpful, unless it is for a service that you actually ask for.

- It is also a good idea to refuse to allow touts to steer you away from public areas, in case your guide plans to rob you (see also scam #29).

- Attracting the tourist police, if there are any, can be any easy way to get rid of the touts, as most of them operate at the margins of legality and want to avoid contact with the law. It is not fool proof, however; with their greater fluency in the local language and practised persuasiveness, they may be able to persuade the policeman that they are harmless and that you are being unreasonable.

My experience of baksheesh in Morocco

Ten years ago, I took the ferry with three friends from Algeciras in Spain to the Moroccan port of Tangier, which American readers can think of as Europe's version of Tijuana. As with so many border towns, its main business is ensuring that passing travellers leave their money with its inhabitants, before they travel to more interesting places in the interior of the country. We had got off the ferry and walked through immigration and customs. We wanted to leave for the spectacular medieval Arab city of Fes that evening, but, in those days before the Internet was everywhere, we had not been able to check the Moroccan train timetables in Spain. Unfortunately it seemed that the last train had already left. We could not, therefore, simply hail a taxi cab to the train station and wait for our train, but needed to find a hotel in Tangier that night.

When we emerged, we saw a number of Moroccans waiting to offer various services to the travellers getting off the ferry. Like a school of predatory fish, they made straight for us. An elderly native targeted us, and somehow seemed to assume that he was our guide. Using what was clearly a well-established routine, and one which would put the best life insurance or car salesman to shame, he seemed to assume that he was finding us a hotel, and acting as our tour guide on the way to the city.

Our guide was clearly trading on our natural politeness to worm his way into our company. As we had no clear idea of where we were going, we were relatively easy meat. He was certainly a very competent hustler, and, while we were aware that he was talking to us because he hoped to get something out of us rather than because he was a genuinely nice person, we could not work out a way to politely get rid of him.

Within an hour, he had steered us to a carpet store and offered to show us a Berber market (see scam #31), and had taken us to a hotel, from which he no doubt extracted a commission later that day (see scam #1). But as well as scamming us in those ways, when he left us, he also demanded a tip from us, and, when we met one demand, kept asking for more. By this time, we simply wanted to get rid of him and unwind after a day of travel, so we met his demands two or three times, but would not meet his fourth, at which point he became rude. Eventually, after a protracted and unnecessarily unpleasant scene, we managed to get rid of him. The money we paid as we parted was baksheesh.

Baksheesh in Suva, Fiji

From an e-mail from a Canadian traveller, 2010:

"There are local wood carvers that wait in Suva city centre for hapless backpackers to come strolling by. They get your attention and sit you down to talk with you. They ask you questions, like your name, where you're from, etc. All the while they are carving a piece of soft wood into a "traditional" Fijian sword, complete with all of the details you just told them about yourself. When they're done speaking with you, they demand that you pay them for the sword they just carved for you. Most people feel guilty enough to fork over some money so as not to offend, even though they never asked for the carving in the first place".

56. Coin swap scam

Likely damage: 1/5

Frequency: 2/5

Countries reported: Mostly Britain and Europe.

Summary: Valuable coins such as the £1 or €2 coins are swapped for foreign coins that are worth much less.

Tourists are usually unfamiliar with the money in the country in which they are travelling, at least during the first few days of their trip. Scammers sometimes exploit this unawareness to short-change them by giving coins as change which look like valuable coins, but are, in fact, worth much less. In order to do so, they must entice the tourist into some form of transaction, perhaps offering postcards for sale, or changing money at favourable rates. The tourist will hand over the valuable coin, and receive the valueless coin in exchange.

The thief can accomplish this exchange in two ways:

- The scammer receives the valuable coin from the tourist for payment, and swaps it for the valueless coin without the victim noticing. He can then say to the tourist, "sorry, you gave me this coin. It is worth nothing. Please pay me again". The tourist may pay again, thereby doubling the scammer's take from the transaction.

- A second way to scam tourists with worthless coins is to include the worthless coin among a stack of valuable coins, while giving change for a note. The scammer may distract the victim by apologising for being forced to give the victim a stack of coins, as he does not have a note to give. This only works if the worthless coin is virtually identical to the valuable coins, otherwise the tourist will be likely to notice that something is wrong.

Tourists in Europe are most vulnerable to this scam, because the euro area and Britain have some of the world's most valuable coins in general circulation. The £2 coin in Britain, for example, is worth $2.50, and the €2 coin is worth only slightly less. Scamming people with coins for change is much less common in the United States, because, with the exception of the unpopular one dollar coins, the most valuable coin is the quarter, which is only worth 25 cents (£0.20). The scammer would need to scam people many times in order to make a noticeable gain, and there are many more lucrative ways to rip people off.

Scams involving substituting worthless coins for British and European change are not confined to Britain and Europe. However, the €2 coin and the British £1 coin are the most likely coins to be swapped for worthless foreign equivalents (see examples below). Any of these coins given as change, should be checked to ensure that they are the genuine article. This advice applies mostly to street vendors and touts in areas frequented with tourists: the likelihood of being given foreign coins as change in supermarkets is much lower.

My experience of coin-swap scammers in Sri Lanka

In Sri Lanka in 2003, I was approached by men who offered to change any pound coins I had on me for five rupee pieces, which look remarkably similar, at an unfavourable rate. They said that I could try and pass the five rupee pieces off for pound coins in London, my next destination. Also in Sri Lanka, men approached me trying to buy pound coins, probably in order to pretend to sell them to tourists for Sri Lankan rupees. At the last moment, they could be swapped for worthless five rupee coins by sleight of hand.

I refused to have anything to do with the swindle.

Two valuable coins and their worthless look-alikes

The following are valuable coins most commonly swapped for coins which are worth considerably less:

- The British one pound coin (being retired in October 2017), worth $1.25, is sometimes swapped for the 1996-2004 Sri Lankan five rupee coin, worth about five US cents. The Sri Lankan coin is no longer being produced, but is still in circulation.

- The two euro coin (see below), worth about £1.80/$2, is swapped for:

-- The old 500 Italian lire coin, worthless since the introduction of the euro in 2002.

-- The five South African Rand coin, worth about 30 US cents.

-- The five Mexican peso coin, worth about 25 US cents.

57. Fake "Good Samaritans" scams

Likely damage: 3/5

Frequency: 1/5

Countries reported: Global.

Summary: Scammers pretend to help tourists, while swindling them. They may try to get hold of their credit cards or ATM PINs, or lead them to an isolated spot and mug them.

Good Samaritans are people who help other people in trouble. Genuine Good Samaritans[1] can literally save travellers' lives, and more commonly can help avoid a significant amount of hassle. Most travellers rely on the unpaid goodwill of a stranger at some point during their travels. This section is about people who offer help, but are in fact out to swindle. Some scams involving people who pretend to help a traveller, but are only out to rip you off, are covered elsewhere in this book. This section notes other common ways in which strangers swindle you while pretending to help. Fake "Good Samaritans" sometimes pretend to be tourists themselves, particularly if their English is good enough, but will usually pose as locals.

Fake "Good Samaritan" scammers will often try to distract victims with valuable possessions while they steal them. In one such scam:

1. A thief and his accomplice will spot a victim driving alone in an expensive rental car or SUV.

2. The scammer will point at the car and wave frantically, trying to attract the victim's attention.

3. If the victim stops and asks the scammer what is wrong, one scammer will say that there is something wrong with the victim's car. He may claim that there is black smoke coming out of the exhaust pipe or that one of the back tires is burst.

4. When the driver tries to get out and look at the back of the car, the scammer will follow him.

5. The scammer's accomplice will get into the unlocked door. If the victim's keys are in the ignition, the accomplice may try to drive off with the car. If there is anything valuable in the car, the accomplice will steal it, and try to get away while the victim is still distracted looking at the back of his car.

In a variant of this scam which seems to be popular in South America:

1. The scammers again target a tourist in a rental car or an expensive SUV.

2. The scammers then sabotage the victim's car, but do not disable it entirely. They may stick a nail in a tire or cut the fuel lines.

3. When the tourist drives away, the scammers follow the car until it stops, then pretend to help the victim while robbing him.

The American embassies in some Latin American countries warn specifically against this scam.

In another variant of this scam:

1. The scammer approaches his victims in the evening in their hotels or in restaurants.

2. The scammer claims that the victim's car, which is parked outside, has been vandalised or broken into.

3. If the victim accompanies the scammer outside with his or her car keys, he robs them and steals the car.

In yet another fake "Good Samaritan" scam:

1. A scammer will target a tourist walking around a city who appears to be lost.

2. The scammer will ask the victim where he wants to go and offer him directions.

3. If the victim tells them, the scammer will say that he happens to be going that way, and that the victim should follow him.

4. The scammer will then lead the victim to a secluded alley or other isolated spot and mug the victim.

With an accomplice, a fake "Good Samaritan" can also perpetrate another swindle involving money:

1. The criminals look for a wealthy looking person, usually female, with valuables on her.

2. One of them starts to mug or assault the victim.

3. The other, the fake "Good Samaritan" intervenes, and attacks the mugger, who is prevented from stealing anything, but manages to get away.

4. The "Good Samaritan" comforts and charms the shocked victim, and persuades her to hand over some cash as a reward.

In another version of that scam:

1. Thieves steal a victim's credit cards.

2. A fake "Good Samaritan" claims that he saw the theft and persuades the victim to call their bank. He claims that he has the bank's phone number. He dials it using his cell phone.

3. In fact, however, he is calling an accomplice (perhaps the mugger who has got away, perhaps yet another scammer). This scammer pretends to be an operator at the bank's call centre. He asks for the victim's account number, credit card number, expiry date and PIN.

4. The scammers then tell the victim that the credit cards have been cancelled and proceed to loot the victim's accounts. The

victim will not discover that she has been swindled in this way until she receives her next credit card bill.

Fake "Good Samaritan" scam at subway ticket machines

In cities with subway systems, tourists often buy expensive weekly passes if they intend to travel frequently by mass transit during their stay. In many cities, these tickets can be bought at ticket machines, and payment made by credit cards. The instructions in the machines, however, are frequently not available in the tourist's language.

1. The scammer hangs around a ticket machine in a station which many tourists use.

2. A tourist has problems using the ticket machine. While the tourist is looking obviously baffled, a scammer will approach and offer to show the tourist how to buy the expensive weekly ticket. When the time comes for payment, he will invite the tourist to put his card in the slot.

3. The scammer will, however, sabotage the transaction somehow, perhaps hitting the "Cancel" button, and it will appear to the tourist that his card does not work.

4. "No matter", the scammer will say, "I will buy a weekly ticket for you and you can pay me in cash". If the tourist agrees, the scammer will turn his attention back to the machine and buy a ticket. He will hand it over to the tourist, and receive the tourist's cash in exchange.

5. The scammer has taken advantage of the tourist's ignorance of the language. The scammer has handed the victim a much cheaper single-journey ticket instead of a weekly pass.

The gain from this scam can be large for a scam that takes a few minutes. In Paris, a single ticket costs €1.90/$2, while a weekly,

Zones 1-5 weekly pass costs almost €22.15. In Rome, a week's pass on the Metro costs €24, while a single use ticket costs only €1.50.

Note:

[1] The name "Good Samaritan" comes from the Bible, specifically the Gospel of Luke, where a man from Samaria helps an injured Jew whom he meets on the road. This would have been shocking to Jesus's Jewish audience, because Samaritans and Jews despised each other.

Chapter 10: Extortion, blackmail and fraud scams

Corrupt policemen and those pretending to be policemen prey on tourists in many countries, especially those in which corruption is endemic. As usual, tourists are particularly vulnerable because they are often unaware of local laws and customs, or even the local language, and usually have more money than locals. Engaging in high-risk behaviour, such as trying to buy drugs or hire a prostitute increases the chances of being scammed in these ways. The criminals exploit the instinct of most of us to obey people in official uniform; most of us will do something we would not otherwise do, when told to by someone we believe to be a policeman.

Policemen can extort effectively because they are in positions of authority. Plenty of other professions with whom tourists deal every day are just as greedy and unscrupulous. This chapter singles out some businesses which rent equipment to tourists, and hotel managers and other employees who keep tourists' passports. These crooks are more insidious than corrupt policemen, but no less greedy.

Finally, travellers can be just as greedy and unscrupulous as any scammer, and scammers can, ironically, take advantage of this.

---

58. Fake policemen scams

Likely damage: 2/5

Frequency: 3/5

Countries reported: Global, in Europe, Central Asia, Thailand and Latin America.

Summary: Scammers dress as policemen, and try to intimidate or trick tourists into giving them money, bank card PINs or other valuables.

In this family of scams, the criminal disguises himself as a policeman, in order to intimidate tourists into handing over their wallets. He will often have an accomplice, since policemen often work in pairs, and two policemen are more intimidating than one. Scams involving policemen or fake policemen who swindle tourists during traffic stops are covered in scam #60, and "on the spot fines" are covered in scam #61.

A common fake policeman scam works as follows:

1. The scammers approach vulnerable-looking tourists.

2. They identify themselves as police, probably flashing fake ID badges, and say that they have had reports of counterfeit money amongst merchants in the area.

3. They may say that many tourists have been duped by money changers, who have given tourists counterfeit local money in exchange for their genuine foreign cash. Could the tourist please hand over his wallet, so that they can check that the tourist is only carrying genuine money?

4. The tourist hands over his wallet. The fake policeman thumbs through it, checking each bill carefully, and apparently replacing them in the wallet. He then hands the wallet back to the tourist, and leaves.

5. When the tourist checks the wallet, however, he will find that the policeman has used sleight of hand to steal the more valuable bills, leaving only the smaller banknotes.

In a slightly more elaborate variant of this scam, a third man is involved:

1. The third man will engage the tourists in conversation, perhaps asking them for directions, or to change money. He will leave.

2. The fake policemen will then come up to the tourists, identify themselves as undercover police, and say that they have been

following the man who approached the tourists. They suspect him of passing counterfeit money. Could the tourists show them their wallets?

3. As before, the tourist hands over his wallet. The fake policeman thumbs through it, checking each bill carefully, and apparently replacing them in the wallet. He then hands the wallet back to the tourist, and leaves.

4. When the tourist checks the wallet, however, he will find that the policeman has used sleight of hand to steal the more valuable bills, leaving only the smaller banknotes.

In another, more sinister, version of this scam, the policemen have an accomplice:

1. The accomplice either tries to sell drugs to the tourists, or plants drugs in their pockets or bags.

2. The "undercover police" then claim that they have been following the man, and have seen him selling drugs to the tourists. They now need to search the tourists for drugs.

3. If the tourists do not consent to the search, they will be arrested and taken to the local police station.

4. When they find the drugs which their accomplice has planted, the fake police will demand a large bribe, or "on-the-spot fine" to let the tourists go – most likely all the cash they have on them.

A different scam involves procedures of identification. In most countries, it is compulsory to carry photo ID. Tourists often do not realise this, or forget their ID at their hotel:

1. Fake policemen therefore know that they can stop tourists and levy "on-the-spot fines" if tourists do not have their passports or photo driving licenses with them.

2. The tourists will most likely pay up, particularly if they are in countries where this form of petty corruption is widespread and notorious.

Not all the police who scam tourists in this way are criminals impersonating police officers. Some of the scammers are real police officers who are simply trying to supplement their salaries. This is rarer in Europe, but there are plenty of reports of this happening in Thailand and Latin America, where the police are badly paid and often corrupt.

Police procedures and powers vary widely around the world, making fake policemen difficult to distinguish from genuine policemen who are extorting bribes or credit card details, who in turn are difficult to distinguish from zealous but honest policemen. In many countries, genuine policemen usually leave tourists alone, while in many others, tourists are routinely harassed by bribe-hungry local cops. Refusing to obey scammers will often make them go away, but refusing to obey genuine policemen can land a tourist in jail. It is therefore difficult to give advice about how to handle fake policemen in every country in the world, though there is plenty of good advice available from the websites of the US State Department or the British Foreign Office about how to act in countries where this scam is a problem. Common tips include:

- Generally, it is advisable to treat policemen in plain clothes who approach you with much more scepticism than their uniformed counterparts.

- Refuse to get into a taxi with policemen who stop you under almost any circumstances.

- Demand to see official identification.

- Refuse to hand over cash unless you are sure that the policeman is genuine.

Indian tourists tricked by fake South African police

Tourists from India fell victim to a group of robbers who pretended to be police officers in Johannesburg in June 2016. According to The Star newspaper, the tourists were travelling in a tour bus when two men, dressed as police offices, stopped the bus and boarded. Two criminals robbed the driver of R800 ($60/£50), and made off with around $700 and four phones from the tourists, before speeding off in an unmarked white VW Polo.

Kim Kardashian, reality TV star, robbed by fake police in Paris

In 2016, celebrity Kim Kardashian West was robbed in Paris by men masquerading as police. The men tied Kardashian West up and locked her in a closet. They stole €10 million ($11 million/£9 million) in jewellery. She was shaken but physically unharmed.

Fake Vietnamese police officer arrested after robbing tourists, Saigon

In Saigon, in 2016, 21-year-old Dang Tuan Thanh and at least two of his accomplices would falsely claim to be police officers in order to check papers and eventually rob victims of cash and phones. As he could speak English, Thanh would dupe his victims into thinking he was a real anti-drug officer. He carried a fake police badge reading, "Certificate Police Office On Drug Crime" [sic].

In one robbery, Dang confronted a 20-year-old British tourist while he was driving his girlfriend home. Dang spoke to them in English, introducing himself as a Vietnamese police officer who needed to check their papers, before forcing them to pay a fine for traffic violations at gunpoint. As he had no money on him, the victim was forced to go with Dang to an ATM booth. The bogus cop eventually fled with cash and the British man's phone. Dang also robbed a Japanese tourist of his phone, and a Dutchman of his electronic devices and cash.

Two Romanian men jailed in London after impersonating police officers

In 2015 and 2016, in London, two Romanian men repeatedly impersonated British police officers in London to rob tourists. The men approached their targets by accusing tourists of crimes before making-off with their possessions. They were caught after a police operation, as they were attempting to rob Chinese tourists. One of the men assaulted police officers as he was being arrested. The men were each sentenced to three years' imprisonment.

Amsterdam fake police scam warning

In 2007, the Dutch police warned tourists visiting Amsterdam to beware of fake policemen who would try to swindle tourists. Fake policemen in plain clothes would flash badges at tourists and demand their cash and credit cards, claiming to be checking for counterfeits. They would sometimes ask for PINs as well.

In fact, Dutch policemen do not carry badges, and plain clothes officers would rarely, if ever, carry out this kind of inspection.

59. Passport extortion

Likely damage: 3/5

Frequency: 2/5

Countries reported: Thailand, Mexico, Venezuela.

Summary: Scammers try to trick tourists into handing over their passports, and then demand money in exchange for the vital document.

This is a fairly common scam in poorer countries with large tourist industries. Though I have not personally been a victim, I have met several people who have. A tourist's passport is, of course, essential for almost all overseas travel (except in some countries, where they will accept ID cards or driving licenses instead), and losing it is usually a major inconvenience. It is very difficult to replace, especially if you are far away from one of your country's embassies, and the time taken to replace it can have a serious knock-on effect on the remainder of your trip (see the example in the introduction to this book).

Thieves know how difficult and costly it can be to replace a passport, and some rely on this fact to scam tourists. Acquaintances of mine have been scammed in this way in Thailand, and I have also heard of it happening in some countries in South America, including Mexico and Venezuela. Scammers often target tourists who rent equipment such as bicycles or diving gear:

1. The tourist attempts to hire some equipment.

2. The shops often ask for a deposit, or a credit card number, but many tourists are understandably reluctant to give credit card information out, since it would be relatively easy for the shop in question to charge their credit card much more than it is entitled to. The tourist would not necessarily find out that the card had been charged for some time.

3. Instead, the shops offer to accept the tourist's passport as a deposit, since it has information in it which can identify the tourist if he does not return the equipment rented, and the cost of replacing the passport is generally higher than the cost of the equipment.

4. When the tourist returns after his cycle ride, or dive, he hands the equipment back, and pays for the rental.

5. The scammers then tell him, however, that there is a "fee" for looking after the passport. The fee is very high and he was not told about it before he rented the equipment. It is not, however, quite extortionate enough for the traveller to refuse: it may be 200 dollars, rather than a couple of thousand or more.

6. If the tourist does not pay the fee, he cannot get the passport back. He then has an unpleasant choice. He can pay the fee, or he can call the police, if there are any. If he calls the police, however, he takes the risk that, even if the police can speak his language, the extortionist may deny everything and he may end up with no passport, or else having to pay a greatly increased fee.

7. The extortionist, of course, counts on him choosing to pay some money, even if not necessarily the full amount originally demanded.

The scam does not necessarily involve a passport. I have heard of wallets, cameras, video cameras and other valuables being demanded as security, and then kept while scammers demand a bribe for their return. It also does not necessarily involve renting equipment. Hotels often ask for, and retain, a guest's passport, if they ask guests to pay bills when checking out, as most do.

Very rarely, hotels also try to extort money from travellers in exchange for their passport, though just because a hotel demands a passport does not mean that they are preparing to swindle their guests in this way.

Ways to reduce the chance of falling victim to this scam are:

- Choose businesses which seem busy and which have been recommended by other travellers. Businesses who deal with locals as much as tourists are also less likely to swindle travellers in this way, though it is not always possible, as few locals in poorer countries stay at expensive hotels or go scuba diving. Busy, popular places, however, are significantly less likely to engage in this form of fraud than empty, impoverished businesses.

- It is certainly better to avoid leaving a passport as security if at all possible. However, many vendors insist on it, and, if a tourist really wants to rent a bicycle in a particular location, it can be difficult to avoid leaving a passport as security. Looking at it from an honest business's point of view, they will want to make sure that the tourist does not walk off with their equipment and not come back, leaving them with a large loss.

- Sometimes, a tourist must leave a passport as security. Some people do not leave their current passport, but leave an expired, and therefore useless, passport as security. Vendors do not usually check whether a passport is expired or not when a tourist leaves it with them. It is often quite easy to hand over this old document. If the business tries to extort some money from a tourist who has left his old passport when he returns the equipment he has rented, or checks out of the hotel, the tourist can simply walk away, and lose only an old passport. (This only works if the victim does not minding losing the stamps in your old passport, which can have considerable sentimental value to some travellers).

- If the vendor is trying to extort money to which he is not entitled from the tourist by retaining the tourist's passport, he will be most unlikely to go to the police, whatever he may claim, to get the money which he says the tourist owes him. Extortion is a serious crime in most countries, and he is unlikely to risk being charged for it.

My experience of passport theft

I have only lost my passport once, in Prague, but that experience was quite enough to make me take better care of it in the future. It was, of course, the night before I was due to catch an early flight home. I was in a bar, put my passport down and turned away to order a drink. When I looked back, it was gone. I had to go to the British embassy the next day and buy a new passport. I also had to rebook my flight home, though fortunately I found a very cheap flight leaving a couple of days later. Had I lost my wallet as well, I would have been in much worse trouble.

60. Police traffic stop scams

Likely damage: 3/5

Frequency: 2/5

Countries reported: Global.

Summary: Policemen or fake policemen stop tourists' cars under a variety of pretexts and rob them or demand bribes.

This family of scams covers policemen or fake policemen who pull tourists over in order to rob them. Fake policemen who scam tourists when they are not driving are covered in scam #58. In every country in the world, law enforcement officials can stop and question drivers if they are breaking the law in some way, for example by not wearing a seatbelt in areas where it is compulsory to do so, by driving without insurance, or by driving with a damaged car. Driving regulations are so complicated that people frequently break them without knowing it in their own countries, and it is much easier to do so abroad. Tourists will rarely study traffic regulations in detail, if at all, when they rent a car. They hope that the rules will be similar enough to those back home that they can risk it for a few days or weeks. Most tourists who risk it in this way are not stopped by the police. Even if they are, as long as the breach of the rules is not too serious, they are often let off with a warning, particularly if the country they are travelling in is dependent on tourists for a large part of its income.

Most people instinctively obey police officers as long as their demands seem reasonable. Scammers know this, and use this instinct to make money from their unsuspecting victims, both locals and tourists. As so often, tourists are more vulnerable, because they often do not know the local language, are rarely familiar with the local laws, and are rarely aware of how to complain.

One such scam has been reported from many countries. It is similar to one of the Good Samaritan family of scams (see scam #57):

1. A police car drives alongside a victim on a rural stretch of road. The victim pulls over, and two fake policemen get out of their car.

2. One policeman knocks on the victim's window, flashes a fake police badge and asks to see the victim's licence. He tells the victim that there was something wrong with his car – perhaps the engine was steaming, his tyre seems flat or the back taillight was not working.

3. The first policeman tells the victim to get out of the car and takes him around to see what the problem was.

4. The fake policeman's accomplice is simultaneously walking around the victim's car. While the victim is absorbed with looking at his engine, tyres or taillights and is talking with the first policeman, his accomplice is busy taking the victim's money and valuables from inside the car.

5. When the first policeman sees that his accomplice has finished robbing the car, he tells the victim that he sees that the car was working after all.

6. The two fake policeman drive off before the victim spots that he has been robbed.

Another scam involves fake policemen who pull the victim over as in the previous scam:

1. The scammers will stop the victim.

2. They will demand to see the victim's licence and insurance, and claim that one or both is not in order. They will say that they are going to have to impound the victim's vehicle.

3. The victim may protest that his insurance is indeed in order, and show them the documentation.

4. The scammers will reply that their computer has said that this vehicle is uninsured. They will threaten the victim with various dire legal penalties if he resists or protests that he is miles from anywhere. They may instruct the victim to appear at the local police station the next day.

5. The scammers give the victim instructions to get back into town, or to catch a bus back to his hotel. They give the victim a place and a time to pick his car up the next day, when the insurance has been sorted out. They even give the victim an official-looking receipt for the car.

6. Reluctantly, the victim leaves the car, taking as many valuables with him as he can. The scammers drive away, and the victim never sees his car again.

Avoiding such scams can be difficult. Local laws are often complicated, and it can be very difficult to tell whether the policeman is honest, but officious; a dishonest but genuine policeman who is demanding a bribe; or a fake policeman. It is not recommended to disobey policemen under any circumstances, unless you are absolutely sure that they are fake. However, here are some tips to reduce the likelihood of becoming a victim of this scam:

- Demanding an identification badge will make many scammers go away, though the better-prepared ones will have forged their own.

- Refusing to pay cash or be separated from your personal property and demanding receipts for any "on-the-spot fines" may make more scammers go away.

- Noting the policeman's badge number will discourage many corrupt officers.

- Unfortunately, any of these suggestions can be inappropriate or even dangerous in some circumstances, and in any such situation, any traveller must play it by ear to a large extent.

Advice from the Hungarian police on being pulled over

The Hungarian police post the following warning on their website (www.police.hu – the somewhat broken English is as in the original webpage):

"There were some cases in Hungary when the disguised criminals acted as a police officer, pretending an official procedure and thus they defraud money from the unsuspecting tourists. These cases rather concern drivers, usually on roads out of town where the traffic is light.

The false police officers always try to get your money. Sometimes they threaten the driver and keep him or her back until he or she pays the demanded amount of money. If you get into a situation like this, always stick to your rights! The most important that you should know is that police officers are not allowed to take over cash as a fine in Hungary. If you are fined on the spot due to the breach of regulations, the police officer has to give you a postal check. If you refuse to receive the postal check or to pay it at the post, the police officer will report you and the competent police authority will carry out the procedure on the offence and will bring a formal decree at the end of the procedure".

Muggings by fake police officers in Nicaragua

The US embassy in Nicaragua advises that Americans are increasingly targeted shortly after arriving in the country by criminals posing as Nicaraguan police officers. These scammers pull over their victims' vehicles – including those operated by reputable hotels – for "inspection". Criminals carrying guns then rob passengers of all valuables and abandon them in remote locations. This activity has been reported on the Tipitapa-Masaya and Managua-Leon Highways. American citizens are warned to be extremely cautious when driving at night from Managua's International Airport and to avoid travelling the Tipitapa-Masaya Highway at night.

Thai and Indian police scams

In some areas in poor countries which see many tourists, such as various Thai islands or Goa in India, the legitimate police have been known to target tourists whom they know will most likely be breaking local traffic laws, whether intentionally or not. They can then levy "on-the-spot fines" and threaten to drag tourists who refuse to pay to jail. In Goa, for instance, it is compulsory for motorcycle riders to wear helmets and carry driving licences. It is a law which was rarely enforced for years, and many locals do not obey it. Locals, however, are less likely to be able to pay a large bribe and it is easy for policemen in Goa, who are very badly paid, to stop helmetless foreigners and demand money to overlook the offence. See example below for a friend's experience of this scam.

In Thailand, policemen have been known to pull foreigners over and demand their driving licences, which are likely to be in their wallets. When the wallet is produced, the policeman grabs it, and takes the tourist's identification out. The policeman then goes back to his car or motorcycle to study the wallet. The policeman steals the cash in the wallet, returns it and denies that there was cash there in the first place.

Indian and Indonesian police extortion

In 2017, I was travelling in the Philippines. I met two young English travellers. One had a friend who was riding a scooter without a helmet in Bali. My friend was on the back with a helmet.

They approached a police checkpoint. The police signalled to them to stop, explaining that, without a helmet, they could cite him and take him to court. The policeman then showed him discreetly a piece of paper with the number 300,000 written on it. The driver took that to mean, correctly as it turned out, that he could pay a bribe of 300,000 Indonesian rupiah (about $22/£19) to avoid being cited. He did so, and they drove away.

The other traveller had a friend who was driving through Goa, India. A police motorbike pulled him over. The policeman demanded 700 Rupees ($10/£8) as a bribe, which, again the person paid to avoid the hassle.

14-year-old police impersonators

In one of the more bizarre of these scams, two 14-year-olds from Florida stole a car and used a blue, flashing police light to stop other drivers. They carried imitation guns and robbed their victims (who were not tourists), demanding money and cigarettes before driving off. They were caught when one of their victims became suspicious and called the real police.

The guns were fakes, but the boys were charged with a number of serious crimes including impersonating a police officer, grand larceny, and robbery with a deadly weapon.

61. "On-the-spot fine" scams

Likely damage: 3/5

Frequency: 2/5

Countries reported: Many, mostly poor countries.

Summary: Policemen pretend that tourists have broken the law and demand thinly-disguised bribes.

Even when their victims are not driving (see scam #60), policemen can often find excuses to extort bribes. Most people who have travelled extensively through poorer countries will have a stock of these experiences, whether first- or second-hand. In many countries, the police are given the power to demand fines which can be paid on the spot for minor offences. In many other countries, they are not allowed to, but do so anyway. And in still other countries, confusingly, an attempt to pay a fine with cash when it is imposed can be treated as bribery, and can therefore land a traveller in serious trouble. As usual, since travellers are relatively rich, and often ignorant of the laws and customs of the country in which they travel, they are often seen as easy pickings for corrupt policemen, or for criminals pretending to be genuine policemen.

If the traveller has committed a genuine offence, however, paying a fake on-the-spot fine to the policeman in cash can work to her benefit. The traveller is paying a scarcely concealed bribe to the policeman for the offence to be forgotten. If drugs are found on her, or if she has been driving drunk, paying a large sum of money, depending on the circumstances, can avoid a huge fine, or months in jail. There is often a complicated etiquette to be observed in such cases, however. In particular, the traveller should never mention the word "bribe", referring instead to "on-the-spot fines" or even a "donation" to a good cause. It is generally helpful to adopt friendly body language, smile, and be as patient as possible.

Many who begin travelling independently in the developing world get a feel for where bribery is ingrained in the culture and where it is likely to get them into serious trouble. Guidebooks often contain advice on the subject, though it is a very treacherous part of travelling and it is impossible to give hard and fast advice about what to do in any situation. Just because bribery is common in one country does not mean it is advisable in its neighbours.

In Chile, for example, bribery is heavily frowned upon, and most of the public officials are impeccably honest. Chile's wealth and honest political culture have allowed it to pay its public officials decently and to punish corruption severely. Cross Chile's northern borders into Peru or Bolivia, however, and the rules of the game change dramatically. Bolivian and Peruvian policemen and other public officials are paid very little, and corruption is tolerated to a far greater extent. Demanding bribes may be inexcusable, but it is easy to understand why a policeman will take the opportunity to double or treble his monthly income by taking a bribe from a tourist whom he catches with a small amount of drugs.

Paying a bribe to avoid trouble may work in a traveller's favour if he has done something wrong, but the flipside is that policemen target tourists to demand bribes, like the Mexican policeman in my example below, even when the tourist has broken no law, or one that is rarely enforced. As with many governmental scams, avoiding corrupt policemen entirely is difficult. If one is targeted in this way, however, there are a number of tactics which can minimise or help avoid this type of extortion if the tourist has not broken the law:

- Asking for a receipt for any fine can discourage the police officer from demanding money, though it can also irritate him, and be more trouble than it is worth.

- Demanding to see his superior, or a consular official from the tourist's embassy can have the same effect, though the policeman's boss may ask for a bribe in addition to the policeman's.

- If there is a tourist police department in the town or city, it can be worth complaining, though in that case, the victim will need the policeman's name and ID number, if any.

All these approaches work best if the tourist is familiar with local laws and the local language, and are only for the patient, as they can result in long and stressful negotiations. Most people end up paying the bribes that are demanded of them, rather than suffer the stress and hassle of negotiating in a foreign country and a foreign language.

My experience of extortion by a Mexican policeman

Many years ago, I was travelling with an American friend through northern Mexico. We had had an interesting night at a few bars in Tijuana. We had not yet been mugged or pickpocketed, nor had we had our drinks spiked, and there was no sign yet of food poisoning from the dinner earlier in the evening. We were in fact feeling fairly pleased that we had avoided any of the scams for which Tijuana is famous. We were heading back to the American border and relative safety.

We were about to get a shock. A policeman stopped us and engaged us in conversation. He seemed amiable enough until he spotted a penknife in my friend's pocket. "This knife is illegal in Mexico, senor", he said. He demanded what he called a "quick fine" of $30, which my friend eventually reduced to $10 as that was almost all the cash he had left. The policeman, of course, "confiscated" the pocket knife, so probably made up the missing $20 by reselling it later, as it was quite a nice one. After about 20 minutes, we were on our way.

Half an hour later, to our relief, we crossed the border back into the United States.

Police extortion in Russia and Africa

In Russia, carrying ID at all times is compulsory, and Russian policemen often demand a tourist's ID and try to find an excuse to extort money. Relatively few Russian policemen speak foreign languages, but this does not seem to prevent them from demanding tourists' money aggressively. The same traditions exist across much of Africa. There, police try to catch criminals by setting up checkpoints at which cars and pedestrians must stop and show identification. In practice, these checkpoints probably cause at least as much crime as they prevent, because many of the police attempt to solicit bribes from locals and travellers. The bribes that the policemen demand are rarely huge, unless they have caught the victim committing a serious crime, but they can add up quickly if the traveller is on a long-distance trip.

62. Rental damage scams

Likely damage: 3/5

Frequency: 2/5

Countries reported: Global, in particular Thailand, Greece, United States, France, Australia, India.

Summary: Car, jet ski or other rental businesses demand compensation for non-existent damage to their equipment, and intimidate tourists if they do not pay up.

This family of scams is a big earner for some businesses which rent goods such as cars, quad bikes, jet skis, bicycles or diving gear, or anything else which is relatively easy to damage and expensive to repair. Companies have worked out a number of ways of making additional money from their customers. They make those who rent this equipment pay for any damage to the items rented. If it is at all valuable, such as a car, this scam can cost the tourist a lot of money. As so often, when it comes to scams by businesses, the dividing line between legitimate extra charges and outright scams is blurred.

One common method of scamming people who rent cars or other valuable and commonly damaged equipment, who are often, though not always, tourists, works as follows:

1. The rental company rents an old car with dents in it, or scratches on it.

2. When the victim returns it, the rental company claims that the pre-existing scratches were not there when the vehicle was rented out.

3. The company then charges the victim for repairing the car, probably, in fact, charging him far more than the repairs actually cost.

4. This scam is particularly effective if the victim has given a credit card as a deposit, because then his card can be charged for the "damage" days or weeks later. As the victim will probably have left the country and will not have evidence that the damage is fake, disputing the charge will be very difficult, and the victim may well conclude that it is not worth the bother.

Even fairly reputable car rental companies sometimes follow this practice. They have been known, for instance, to charge a customer for filling the fuel tank after the customer returned the car, though the customer had filled the tank just before bringing it back. Since they often charge customers extra for fuel, beyond the usual per gallon prices and for the labour involved in filling up the tank, this can be quite expensive, though it is rarely a huge amount of money. Often, however, the first the customer will find out about this will be when she scrutinises her credit card bill weeks later; as with disputing the pre-existing damage on the car, it is usually impossible to prove that she returned the car with its fuel tank full. Car rental companies have also been known to charge customers for broken mirrors which were already broken when the car was rented, and for bumpers which were already missing.

To avoid being scammed by car or other rental businesses, it is important to take the following steps:

- Inspect the equipment before renting it, looking in particular for any dents, cracks, blemishes or other imperfections.

- Note any problems, and insist that the rental company gives you a written record of them. Do not accept any excuses. If you are renting with somebody else, ensure that he inspects the equipment with you and show him any imperfections.

- It is advisable, though probably unrealistic, to read the long and detailed contracts which are used in car rentals, insisting that the employee you are dealing with draws your attention to the important points of the contract, and the areas which might make you liable to pay more. Some people who report that rental companies have scammed them would have avoided the unpleasant experience they have suffered had they read their contract thoroughly.

- Inspect the equipment after the rental with an employee of the rental company, and have him highlight any problems he finds, in front of a witness or a video camera if possible.

- Always return a rental car with the fuel tank full, if possible, and *keep* the receipt from the fuel station.

- When paying by credit card, check the first bill after renting the equipment for any unauthorised or unfair charges. Do not be afraid of disputing them with the credit card company.

- Never leave your current passport as security for a rental if you can avoid it (see scam #59).

- If possible try and use busy rental companies used by locals rather than just tourists.

These steps will not avoid all scams by rental companies, but should reduce significantly your chance of falling victim to one or more of them.

British cabinet minister caught in car rental scam

One widely-publicised example of a car rental company ripping off a customer by claiming for non-existent damage was the experience of Ruth Kelly, the former British Secretary of State for Transport. According to the London Evening Standard (11 September 2009), she was charged £1,180, or around $2,000 at the exchange rate of the time, "for damage" to a vehicle she had rented. The tires had gone flat less than an hour into the journey. She had returned the fuel tank full, but was also charged for some petrol.

After The Standard intervened, Europcar said in a statement: "Europcar is sorry for the inconvenience to Ms Kelly and the delays in receiving a response from our customer service team. With regard to charges made for the tyres and the fuel, we have liaised with our colleagues in France and can confirm the charges were made in error. We have therefore refunded Ms Kelly. We have also refunded the cost of the rental as a gesture of goodwill". Whether Ms Kelly would have received a refund if she was not a famous person with a large circulation newspaper on her side, is unclear.

Quad bike rental scam on Greek islands

On some Greek islands, tourists use quad bikes to ride around the beaches. Some of the rental companies deliberately under-price the rental of the quad bikes, in order to get as much business from the tourists as possible. The companies count on tourists damaging the bikes to some extent, as they can then charge their customers extortionate amounts for repairing them. Only in this way can they make a profit on renting the bikes. This might be above-board if they stated upfront that people who rent their equipment are likelier than not to have to pay for damaging it, and provided, on request, a list of the charges which their customers are likely to face. However, as the companies plan on luring tourists in and then hitting them with as many concealed charges as possible, this practice more than meets the definition of a "scam".

Pattaya jet-ski extortion scam exposed

In 2009, a British documentary, Big Trouble in Tourist Thailand, showed some Royal Marines, fresh from a tour in Afghanistan, trying to return jet-skis they had rented on Pattaya beach. A Marine Police Sergeant arrived and defused the situation after exposing the jet-ski owner as an extortionist. The Marines eventually paid around $1,000 (then £600). Consular officials recorded more than 100 cases of this scam on Ko Samui in one three month period. This scam is so widespread in Thailand that some sources advise not renting jet-skis there at all. If you do, and face extortion, the same sources advice avoiding the police, who claim a share of the take.

63. Prostitute blackmail scams

Likely damage: 4/5

Frequency: 2/5

Countries reported: Global.

Summary: The oldest profession steals its customers' information and blackmails them.

Some travellers go on holiday specifically for the opportunities for commercial sex, and others feel able to enjoy this form of entertainment when they are thousands of miles from home. This book makes no judgement on the morality, or otherwise, of prostitution between consenting adults. It does cover blackmailing and theft by prostitutes, however, because travellers are so often the victims of scams by prostitutes, "escorts", "masseuses" and the like. There are many dangers to which anyone using a prostitute is exposed, besides those related to deliberate scamming. The risk of contracting an infectious disease, for example, can be extremely high.

Being caught by legitimate police officers in places where prostitution is illegal is also a danger.

Prostitutes and their pimps have been blackmailing both visitors and locals for centuries, or even longer. People may pay for sex in every country in the world, but it is illegal, or at least considered shameful, in most of them, creating an obvious opportunity for blackmail. Many men who use prostitutes are married, making them good targets for extortion. In many of the countries where prostitution is banned, it is quietly tolerated as long as it is kept to certain areas of towns and times of the night. Even where it is legal or semi-legal, it is often controlled by organised criminals. Opportunities for scamming travellers are almost unlimited, especially as they are less likely to be aware of local laws than locals.

One well known scam plays on the client being distracted during sex:

1. The prostitute invites the victim back to her room.

2. The client takes his clothes off, and begins to have sex with her.

3. While the victim's attention is otherwise engaged, an accomplice somehow steals his identification (and possibly his money as well).

4. If the client has a wife, he can then be blackmailed by the criminals, who will threaten to reveal his actions. If the criminals are particularly organised, the room may be rigged with a hidden camera of some sort, to obtain proof of the husband's infidelity, which they can then send to his wife (or children or colleagues) if he does not pay up.

Another, similar, scam, does not rely on the victim being married. It works best in countries where prostitution is punished with heavy penalties:

1. The prostitute invites the victim back to her room.

2. The client takes his clothes off, and begins to have sex with her.

3. The scammers surprise the victim in the act, or just afterwards.

4. Rather than threatening to tell the victim's wife that he has used a prostitute, criminals may threaten to go to the police.

5. The victim will be much more frightened if the scammers can produce convincing evidence of the transaction, such as photographs or recordings.

6. In practice, of course, it may be unlikely that the blackmailers will send the evidence to the police, as they will not want to attract police attention to their scam, but the victim, pulling up his trousers, will be unlikely to refuse to pay.

A further scam, which can work on travellers who believe prostitution is illegal, runs as follows:

1. The victim engages a prostitute in his hotel room.

2. The scammers fake a police raid on the hotel.

3. While the terrified victim reaches frantically for his clothes and mumbles an unconvincing explanation, the fake policemen can extort bribes from him, perhaps in the guise of "on-the-spot fines" (see scam #61).

4. If the victim refuses to pay, he may be beaten up or threatened. He is unlikely to complain to the tourist police even if he suspects that the police raiding his room are not what they appear to be, since he believes that prostitution is a crime.

Blackmail by a prostitute or their confederates is often much more effective if the prostitute, as well as the victim, is male (see the example below). In many countries where female prostitution is tolerated, gay sex is considered a serious crime, even when no money changes hands. This makes blackmail much more effective, especially if the victim cannot identify the prostitute. Gay travellers need to pay much more attention to local laws and customs before engaging a prostitute.

These, or similar, scams have been reported from many countries, and, as mentioned above, affect locals as well as travellers. Countries where such swindles appear to be particularly widespread and to target travellers specifically include Cuba, Thailand and Tunisia. Even avoiding prostitutes altogether will not always stop these scams. In some countries, talking to women in bars can put a traveller in danger of blackmail, because, for instance, the woman may only reveal that she is a prostitute once the fake "police" have appeared.

There are steps which the traveller can take, which can reduce the risk of being blackmailed by prostitutes:

- It is important to be aware of the law regarding prostitution, and if possible to find out how rigorously it is enforced.

- In the few countries where brothels are legal, it can be safer to use a reputable one than cruising for a call-girl on a street. Using a legal brothel can also reduce the risk of contracting a sexually transmitted disease.

- It is much safer for the client to meet a prostitute at his accommodation rather than hers, though it is far more dangerous for the prostitute and many will refuse so-called "outcalls".

- Hiding your identification will reduce the risk of being blackmailed.

Gay Finnish man kidnapped in Thailand after soliciting a prostitute

In Pattaya, in Thailand, a Finnish man invited a male prostitute back to his apartment for sex. Gay prostitution is legal in Thailand, and the prostitute was above the age of consent. The two men hired a motor taxi. Suddenly, the taxi was stopped by an unmarked car and six men, including two police sergeants, got out. They demanded 700,000 Baht (then around $17,000/£10,000) from the Finn, threatening to take him to a police station for formal charging and finger-printing. They imprisoned him and his escort in a hotel room until they could raise the money. The man told to guard the room, however, fell asleep and the escort raised the alarm at the police station. The real police arrived, and released the Finn. The man who had been guarding the hotel room was arrested; two police sergeants were sought for questioning, and three Burmese men were suspected of involvement.

64. Injured relative scam

Likely damage: 3/5

Frequency: 2/5

Countries reported: India, Thailand.

Summary: Scammers get hold of tourists' details and call their next of kin, pretending that the tourist has been injured or arrested, and demanding money to get them out of trouble.

This scam does not target travellers directly. Instead, it targets their friends and families. It is similar to the e-mail scam in which the scammer contacts the victim's friends and family, purporting to be the victim, who has been ill, and demands money to settle medical bills (see scam #59).

For this scam, however, the criminal does not need access to the victim's e-mail account:

1. The scammer obtains the victim's home address and the names and phone numbers of his next of kin. He can do this if he has sight of the victim's passport, on the back page of which next of kin are often listed as emergency contacts.

2. Another way is to bribe a tour company: travellers often have to list their emergency contacts when they sign up to tours with an element of danger, such as white-water rafting or canyoning.

3. The scammer then contacts the victim's friends and family. He pretends to be a doctor at a hospital, and says that the victim has been injured. He may ask for the victim's credit card details, or for money for the victim's medical treatment to be cabled to a bank account which he names.

4. The fake doctor will say that the money has to be sent urgently, otherwise the traveller's treatment will have to stop.

5. If challenged, the scammer will invent a reason why the traveller's travel insurance does not cover the costs of hospitalisation.

6. The victims will never see the money again.

In another variant of this scam:

1. As above, the scammer obtains the victim's home address and the names and phone numbers of his next of kin.

2. The scammer calls the traveller's family and pretends to be a police officer from the country where the traveller currently is. In order to boost his credibility, the scammer may give official-sounding, but fake, contact details, such as names and addresses, of hospitals or police stations.

3. They will say that the traveller has been arrested and needs either the victim's credit card details or a substantial sum of money to be wired as bail, or perhaps as a fine, to an account they designate.

4. Again, they will control the account, and disappear with the money.

Criminals trying to scam people in this way often prefer to phone their victims late at night. This means that their victims will probably be woken up by their phone calls and therefore their resistance will be lower and they will be likely to hand over the money more easily. Scammers are also more likely to target relatives, in particular parents, of younger travellers, such as students or gap year travellers, whose parents will be more likely to pay up without difficulty.

To avoid becoming a victim of this scam:

- Refuse to give out the names and addresses of your next-of-kin to anyone who has no obvious need for them.

- Tell your next-of-kin about this scam, and to refuse to wire money to accounts which they do not recognise. They should be very suspicious of requests from overseas for money, and should not send their credit card details to a third party, unless they have been able to verify that the third party is who they claim to be. The Internet has made it much easier to find the names and addresses of police stations and hospitals overseas.

- If you are contacted by someone asking for money on behalf of a friend or relative overseas, the best advice is to ask for the phone number and other contact details of the person who is calling, and then say that you will call back. Verify as many of the contact details either online or over the phone as possible, and if you are in doubt, ask for more information which you can check yourself.

65. Tourist kidnapping

Likely damage: 5/5

Frequency: 1/5

Countries reported: Global, but in particular India, Venezuela, Pakistan, Afghanistan, Mexico, Colombia, the Philippines,

Panama, South Africa, West Africa, Yemen, Dominican Republic, Nigeria.

Summary: In many countries, tourists are targeted for kidnap and ransom, either for political or financial reasons.

Kidnapping for ransom is, mercifully, extremely rare in most countries. In some parts of the world, however, it is much more common. At its best, it is a horrifying ordeal for the victim, and it can often be fatal, either because the kidnappers decide they have no more use for their hostage, or, occasionally, because a rescue attempt ends badly.

Some people distinguish between three types of kidnapping from which tourists may suffer. In the first, and usually least expensive type, the tourist is seized and forced to withdraw money from an ATM. These so-called "ATM abductions" are covered in scam #22. Though the victim will also lose any valuables and cash which they may have on them, the nightmare is, at least, usually over in a few hours.

Suffering an ATM abduction is traumatic enough, but "express kidnappings", or "quicknappings" are far worse. The kidnapper abducts a victim and negotiates with family members or his travel insurance company for a ransom. The idea with an express kidnapping is not to make the maximum ransom possible, but to get a fairly large sum of money quickly from the victim's family, without long and dangerous negotiations. The kidnappers may injure their victims while they hold them to persuade the victim's family to pay the ransom quickly. The victim is again usually released after payment.

Express kidnappings seem to occur most frequently in some countries in Latin America, including Mexico, Brazil, Venezuela and Ecuador. This particular type of kidnapping is almost certainly under-reported: it may be that as many as 90 per cent of these crimes are not notified to the police. A 2005 Venezuelan film, Secuestro Express (Express Kidnapping), highlighted the growing problem in that country (though the film was criticised by the government and the director was prosecuted).

In a third type of kidnapping, the kidnappers plan to hold the victim over the long term. They will have prepared a hiding place which is difficult to find, such as the basement of an abandoned building or a shack in a remote village in a tribal area. They will issue demands and expect to negotiate. Being held in this way places great physical and psychological demands on a victim. Because of the danger and the amount of preparation involved, the kidnappers will expect a large ransom if they want money, or significant concessions if their motives are political.

The brief summaries of kidnappings in the examples below cannot do justice to the terror and stress that the victims and their families suffer. The websites of the American State Department, the British Foreign Office, and the Australian Department of Foreign Affairs all have country summaries which say whether the country you are visiting has a bad record for kidnappings:

- Most obviously, exercise extreme caution in areas where kidnapping is common, or, if possible, avoid them altogether.

- Even in areas where economic kidnapping is most common, tourists are less likely to be kidnapped if they avoid looking conspicuously wealthy, dress modestly, and leave their expensive Rolexes or $5,000 cameras back at the hotel.

- Kidnappings often take place in unlicensed taxis, and tourists should avoid taking them if possible. Travellers should always be aware of their surroundings, especially when using an ATM.

- Tourists are much less likely to be kidnapped in crowded, well-lit areas than in lonely, dark alleyways. Settling into a routine when you are in a foreign city makes you more vulnerable to kidnappers.

In the extremely unlikely event that the worst comes to the worst, and you are kidnapped while travelling, the US State Department gives some advice about what to do. Points include:

- Do not fight but give the kidnappers what they want. You are more valuable than your cash or your watch.

- Consider carefully before attempting escape, since most attempts fail. You may be terrified, but resistance is likely only to make your kidnappers more hostile.

- If you are kept for a long time, try and maintain your physical and mental health.

Two Canadians kidnapped and murdered by Filipino terrorists

In an extremely distressing case, two Canadian and one Norwegian tourists were kidnapped for ransom by Filipino terrorists of the Abu Sayyaf group on the southern island of Mindanao in 2015. The kidnappers demanded a ransom of several million dollars for the Canadians. The Canadian government refused to pay. The men were murdered in June 2016. The Norwegian was ransomed, and was released.

Australian man kidnapped and raped British tourist

In March 2017, an Australian man was charged with kidnapping and raping a female British tourist. After the pair met at a party in Cairns, he was alleged to have held her against her will and driven her around Australia, before the 22-year-old victim managed to get away and raise the alarm. At the time of writing, the case is continuing.

Three kidnapped at the Rio Olympics

Three Swedish tourists, in Rio during the 2016 Olympic Games, were kidnapped when they asked their Uber driver to stop so that they could take some photos. As they were doing so, criminals approached them and demanded that the Swedes go with them. The Uber driver fled the scene and reported the incident. The police mounted an operation and rescued the tourists, who were fortunately unharmed.

66. Distracting and mugging travellers

Likely damage: 3/5

Frequency: 5/5

Countries reported: Global.

Summary: Something unpleasant is sprayed on a traveller. The scammer moves to brush it off, and while doing so picks the victim's pockets.

The "Distraction" scam is so popular with scammers around the world that it can really be considered global. It is frighteningly simple and effective, and, while locals as well as travellers can be victims, enough travellers suffer from it so that it merits inclusion in this book. It can overlap with the Fake "Good Samaritan" family of swindles (see scam #57). There are an infinite number of varieties of this scam, but a typical version runs as follows:

1. The victim is in a busy, public place in a foreign country. She could be strolling around or sitting and reading a book.

2. The scammer attempts to engage his victim in conversation. He may squirt ketchup on her, then apologise and make as if to rub it off. He may offer his victim worthless souvenirs and urge her to buy them.

3. While the victim is distracted, the scammer's accomplice will go through the victim's bags or pockets or both, stealing anything of value, or possibly simply running away with bags which his victim has put down around her.

4. When the scammers are finished, they lose themselves in the crowd, and the victim never sees either of them, or her valuables, again.

Thieves and pickpockets flourish in places where people are carrying valuables such as cameras or wallets with lots of cash, and are distracted. The person who holds the victim's attention does not have to be directly involved in the scam. People watching street performers are often targeted by pickpockets. Women are particularly vulnerable, since they often carry valuables in handbags or purses, whose straps can be cut easily. They are also less likely to challenge muggers, and less likely to succeed if they do so.

The most obvious way to avoid losing lots of valuable possessions to this scam is to follow the advice often given to tourists in foreign countries and carry only those valuables that are likely to be needed for the day. Valuables left either in the hotel safe, or suitably concealed in a hotel room, are much less likely to be stolen (or damaged, or broken) – though it is still possible that they will not be there when you get back. It is not always possible for a tourist to leave all his valuables there. One is almost certain to need cash for the day, and in some developing countries, acceptance of credit cards is patchy at best.

In many countries, it is compulsory to carry some form of ID, such as a passport or a driver's licence, in case you are stopped by the police. A tourist is also likely to need a camera or camcorder, and maybe a laptop. If he is catching a bus or a flight, he will have to take everything with him, which is why so many muggers target tourists at bus and train stations. Airports are usually safer for tourists than other areas of a country because they are so heavily policed, though it is still possible to be robbed there, especially in the arrivals area after customs.

Knowing whether the area the traveller is visiting is particularly bad for muggings can be useful. Guidebooks, travellers' websites such as the excellent Lonelyplanet.com, and word of mouth from other tourists are all useful sources for tips on which areas are prone to this kind of crime and which are not.

Advice from guidebooks can be out-of-date, however, as they are often researched and published years before. Some places which previously had a bad reputation for pickpockets and muggings, such as the area around New York's Times Square, have improved dramatically in recent years, while others, such as parts of Buenos Aires, have become more violent and crime-infested over the same period.

A variant of the distraction scam takes place in a hotel suite, which needs to have at least one room as well as the bedroom (for example, an en-suite bathroom or a sitting room):

1. The victim's possessions are scattered around the room. There is a knock on her door. She opens it, and the scammer walks in.

2. The scammer is dressed as a plumber, or other maintenance man. He tells the victim that he has heard of a problem with the plumbing in her bathroom (or with the electricity in the sitting room, if the victim has a large suite), and has been sent by the hotel to fix it. Could the victim please show him the bathroom?

3. He walks into the other room with the victim, and asks her whether she has noticed any leaks or funny smells. The victim does not realise, however, that the scammer has left the front door to the suite unlocked.

4. While the scammer and the victim are talking in the other room, the scammer's accomplices enter the main room and steal the victim's valuables. The fake plumber may well turn the taps or the shower on to muffle the sound of the theft.

5. Eventually, the fake plumber leaves, and the victim goes back into the bedroom. The scammers will hope that the victim does not notice she has been robbed until they are clear.

There are certain measures a traveller can take to prevent his valuables being stolen, if he is going to a place with a bad reputation for thefts:

- Cameras or camcorders should not be held dangling on strings. A thief can easily cut them with a knife if the tourist is not paying attention.

- Travellers are often advised to use money belts, which keep money, cards and a passport almost invisible under the shirt, though some thieves have trained themselves to be able to detect and steal them. I have never used a money belt, but instead keep my wallet in an inside pocket of my jacket, if I am wearing one. If not, I make sure it is bulging with coins, and keep it in a front trouser pocket where I can feel it immediately if it is being stolen. Because my wallet is so fat, stealing it from my trouser pocket would be no easy matter, though taking it out to pay for something is difficult too!

- Other advice commonly given to travellers to avoid being mugged is to be "aware of their surroundings", especially in crowds, without being paranoid, and letting the fear of being mugged ruin their trip. In concrete terms, being aware of your surroundings means, for instance, trying not to be lost, and if you are lost, not seeming lost. Don't peer at a map every few yards. This is particularly important in poorly lit areas at night. Thieves love darkness: the cover that it gives them lets them steal and then escape. It also means keeping an eye on anyone who is keeping an eye on you, especially if he is a young man, like the vast majority of muggers. It is useful to know where the nearest policeman is, and to be aware what the words for "Stop, thief!" and "Help!" are in the local language.

Man robbed by "Good Samaritan" in Sydney

A 50-year-old man went to an ATM in Sydney, Australia. He then walked down George Street in the centre of the city, and suddenly noticed that his clothes were damp. A "Good Samaritan" offered to help him dry them, and the pair went to a pub. After a short time on top of a heater, the clothes were dry. The two men parted. Later, however, the victim noticed that "Good Samaritan" had removed his wallet from the clothes while they were drying. The wallet contained the cash he had just withdrawn from the ATM.

My mugging in Tijuana, Mexico

I had visited Tijuana, the famously dangerous town just on the Mexican side of the US-Mexico border, one night. I was walking back towards the American border with a friend. We were less than a mile from the frontier crossing. A group of about ten young children approached us. One of them offered me a bunch of flowers, while the others ran their hands through my trouser pockets. Fortunately, I had only my wallet in those pockets, and was able to grab it before it was removed. My passport and my camera were in the inside pocket of my jacket. Eventually, my friend and I chased them off. The oldest child could not have been more than eight, so they had probably been taught what to do by an adult, or possibly by older children. As these children were all below the age of criminal responsibility in Mexico, they could not be punished for their crimes, and could not, therefore, be forced to reveal who had taught them to scam in this way, in exchange for a lighter sentence.

As so often on that particular border, crossing back into the United States was a huge relief.

Epilogue: How I try to avoid being scammed

The scams described in this book may seem a fairly comprehensive list of all the ways in which travellers are swindled before and during their trips. But there are plenty of other scams out there, and new tricks are emerging all the time. So here are a dozen pointers which I use to keep myself safe while travelling. These tips have not protected me completely from being swindled. I think, however, that they have protected me at least to some extent:

1. If an offer looks too good to be true, it probably is, so I usually pass. This applies anywhere, from advertisements in newspapers or online to offers from touts in bus stations.

2. I do not accept food or drink from strangers whom I have just met in hotels or on buses or trains.

3. I pay careful attention to my surroundings when using an ATM. I try to guard my PIN carefully, and avoid being distracted while using the machine.

4. Before I travel, I do at least a little research to find out whether my destination is notorious for any particular scams. I find that embassy websites and online travel forums are particular good sources.

5. I watch my taxi drivers like a hawk. Many are honest, but many will cheat given the slightest chance.

6. If I do not need to carry something valuable when I go out, I leave it in my hotel. If necessary, I ask the management to put it in the hotel safe.

7. I try to learn something about the currency I will have to use at my destination. I find out the exchange rate before I go, and I try and familiarise myself with notes and coins as soon as possible.

8. I try to keep as many of my possessions as possible in my sight when I am out and about.

9. I do not always assume that policemen or customs officials are honest, especially in poorer countries.

10. I carry a backup ATM or credit card with me in case I lose my main card. Having been broke in a foreign city, I would rather not repeat that experience.

11. I try not to arrive in foreign cities after dark. Thieves love darkness.

12. I do not buy expensive goods overseas unless I know exactly what I am doing.

Above all, though, *I do not let worrying about being scammed ruin my trip*, any more than I let the possibility of being run over stop me crossing the road!